A NIGHT IN OCTOBER

A Suspense Play

by

MAURICE CALLARD

(A radio version of this play
has been broadcast by the BBC.)

**NEW PLAYWRIGHTS' NETWORK
35, SANDRINGHAM ROAD,
MACCLESFIELD,
CHESHIRE. SK10 1QH**

CHARACTERS

MABEL

ROBERT

ANN

PETER

RUTH

491190115

The action passes in the living — room of the Thurlows' house in Sutton.

ACT ONE Scene 1.   An October evening.
             Scene 2.   Breakfast — time the following morning.

ACT TWO Scene 1.   A few moments later.
             Scene 2.   An hour later.

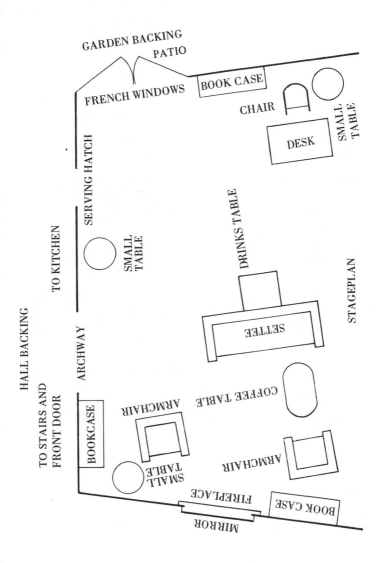

A NIGHT IN OCTOBER

PRODUCTION NOTES

Technically this is a straight-forward play to stage; its appeal depending on the situation and the twists of the plot.

Ann, Ruth and Mabel, although sisters are contrasting characters.

MABEL is inclined to be "hay-wire" and she is not the sort of person that one could rely upon in a crisis.

RUTH is a passionate, earthy creature. This should be emphasised in her scenes with PETER. In her scenes with ANN her jealousy — even her bitterness towards her sister — should be subtly hinted at.

ANN should be charming and ought to get the sympathy of the audience throughout.

PETER has worked very hard to achieve a position of prominence in his profession. This success has made him snobbish. He has won so much that he has such a lot to lose. This is what makes him appear less loving to his wife at times than perhaps he ought to be.

ROBERT is a desperate man, putting everything on one last effort to prove his son's innocence. This makes him appear ruthless for most of the time. But there are one or two occasions when he loses his 'cool' and at the end he is much distressed at the havoc he has caused in the household.

A NIGHT IN OCTOBER

ACT ONE
SCENE ONE

THE SCENE *is the living-room of the Thurlows' house near Sutton. It is a bookish room and there is a desk with papers and books U.L.C. In L. wall there are french windows opening onto a patio and garden. R. of C. in the back is an archway giving onto a hall which, one way leads to the front door of the house and to the stairs and the other way to the kitchen. There is a serving hatch in L. side of back wall. The furniture is substantial, leather-upholstered and comfortable and, with the pictures and ornaments, reflect the pedagogic character of the owner.*

The room is in darkness, the darkness of an October evening, made more gloomy by the approach of a thunderstorm, the first rumblings of which can be heard. A key scratches in the lock of the front door and a light is put on in the hall.

MABEL: *(off; sounding very concerned)* Can you manage?
ROBERT: *(off)* Yes, I'm all right. *(A gasp of pain).*
MABEL: *(off)* Be careful! Don't slip on that rug.
ROBERT: *(off)* I'll manage.
MABEL: *(off)* Here! Lean on me.
ROBERT: *(off)* No, no. It's not that bad.
(As she enters the room MABEL puts her hand to the switch and the lights in the living-room come on. She is flustered and anxious and is vaguely helping ROBERT who is limping and grimacing with pain. She pilots him into the room.)

MABEL: Come over here. *(Leading him to C.)*

ROBERT: Ooh! My elbow's sore. *(He rubs it.)*

MABEL: Sit down. *(Indicates settee C.)* Here.

ROBERT: *(painfully sitting and stretching out his right leg)* I twisted my ankle a bit when I fell. And my elbow. *(He rubs it and indicates how painful it is)* The car must have caught me there.

MABEL: I didn't hit you hard, did I? A glancing blow.

ROBERT: *(shaking his head as if to clear it)* I feel shaken more than anything.

MABEL: *(in an effort to convince herself)* You're bound to. But you'll be all right.

ROBERT: *(looks up at her quizzically)* Yes. Yes, I expect so.

MABEL: *(trying to be bright)* I'll get you a drink. I reckon you could do with a drink. *(Moves to drinks trolley U.R.)*

ROBERT: Good idea!

MABEL: *(halting suddenly)* Oh! Wait a minute! Are you supposed to have strong drink after an accident?

ROBERT: Have you got brandy? I should think brandy'll be all right.

MABEL: Brandy? Yes. *(She pours brandy and brings it down to him.)* There!

ROBERT: Thanks.

MABEL: I need one, too. *(She goes to trolley and pours herself a very generous brandy.)*

ROBERT: A bit distressing for both of us!

MABEL: *(moving down slightly towards him)* It wasn't my fault, you know.

ROBERT: *(blandly)* Oh! Wasn't it?

MABEL: No. You must admit that.

ROBERT: I got knocked over by your car. That's all I know.

MABEL: I'd slowed right down. I was about to turn into the drive. Then you stepped out right in front of me. I didn't stand a chance of . . . .

ROBERT: I can't remember exactly how it . . . .

MABEL: You seemed to jump out. And then jump back again. I hardly hit you at all. Good job I wasn't going any faster.

ROBERT: I'm still trying to fathom how it could have happened. *(Slight pause)* I can't even be sure what I was doing in this road. *(He glances up into her face. She shifts uncomfortably under his stare.)* I had a job to do, someone to visit.

MABEL: You can't remember who?

ROBERT: *(still staring at her)* Someone around here. It must have been. *(He looks away from her and appears to be concentrating)* I came down by train. And took a cab at the station. Then I dismissed it at the end of the road because I knew I would have to search for the house. I'd been given the address and it was while I was walking along that . . . .

MABLE: There you are! You were probably thinking about finding the house and . . . . I mean, that's why you walked out in front of me.

ROBERT: *(after considering this for some time)* I suppose so.

MABEL: *(after a pause)* Well, thank God, you're not hurt more.

ROBERT: *(peeved by this)* I'm hurt enough.

MABEL: *(disconcerted because she has upset him a bit)* Come on, drink your brandy. And rest for a while. You'll soon feel better. *(She stands by him watching him sip his brandy. Then tentatively, nervously almost:)* I don't think you'll want a doctor, will you?

ROBERT: *(gives her a long, straight look)* A doctor? *(pause)* No, perhaps not. Well, I hope not. *(He looks about the room with a more than casual interest)* You don't live here alone?

MABEL: Oh, no. My sister and . . . .

ROBERT: Your sister! What about your husband?

MABEL: *(perplexed)* My husband? What about . . . ?

ROBERT: He's not here?

MABEL: No, he's not. Buy why should you . . . ?

ROBERT: It's just as well. We can come to an arrangement, then.

MABEL: An arrangement! About what? (ROBERT *is staring at her face. She is a little frightened.)* The accident? Why should I? It wasn't my fault.

ROBERT: Oh, forget about the accident.

MABEL: Forget it? *(puzzled and worried)* Then what arrangements are you talking about?

ROBERT: *(rises painfully; looking at her steadily with a hint of contempt)* I've been wondering what you looked like.

MABEL: *(baffled)* Me? Why should you?

ROBERT: *(moving U.R. to cut off any possible flight into the hall)* Oh, I've been told a lot about you. What a gay sort you are . . . . or were.

MABEL: *(now frightened)* You're not well.

ROBERT: Don't you worry about me. I'm all right.

MABEL: *(after watching him for some moments)* You're threatening me somehow. I'm going to get the Police. *(She moves to the telephone on the desk, L, and then realises that this is the one thing she dare not do. As she stands indecisively with the hand-set in her hand ROBERT moves across quickly and checks her.)*

ROBERT: No. *(Taking the hand-set from her and replacing it on its cradle)* No, we don't want the Police in on this. Not yet, anyway.

MABEL: *(backing D.L.)* I don't understand at all. Who are you? And what do you want with me?

ROBERT: Go and sit down. *(He indicates chair below French windows, D.L. MABEL reluctantly sits there.)* I can see I shall have to begin by making things crystal clear to you. *(pause)* Got *any* idea who I am?

MABEL: I've never seen you before. I'm sure of that.

ROBERT: *(somewhat aggresively, impatiently)* Come on, look at me. (MABEL *raises her eyes to him)* Don't I remind you a bit of someone you knew . . . . someone you knew very well indeed . . . . a year ago?

MABEL: A year ago! What happened a year ago?

ROBERT: To be exact the night Miss Carstairs died. The night she was murdered. Now don't tell me you don't remember that.

MABEL: Miss Carstairs?

ROBERT: *(with growing impatience)* Oh, come on. She lived quite near here. In the Crescent . . . No. 87 . . .

MABEL: Oh, *that* Miss Carstairs.

ROBERT: *(sarcastically mimicking her)* Yes, *that* Miss Carstairs.

MABEL: I heard about the murder. And I remember reading about the trial later.

ROBERT: Did you ever see a photograph of the man they accused?

MABEL: I might have done. I don't know.

ROBERT: Oh, you'd have remembered if you had.

MABEL: What are you getting at?

ROBERT: *(Rather dramatically turns his back on her and moves to R.C.)* That young man got life — for a murder he didn't commit. *(Swings round to face her; accusingly)* And you knew he didn't do it . . . . couldn't have done it. If you'd been brave enough to tell the Police at the time you could have saved him. But that case isn't closed yet. Because before I leave here you're going to tell me all you know.

MABEL: *(rising)* I swear I've no idea what you're talking about. *(They stand staring at one another for a few moments. ROBERT is excited but composed. MABEL is nervously fidgetting. At last:)* Look, I've got to put the car away — before my sister gets back — or there'll be trouble. *(She waits for permission as it were.)*

ROBERT: *(with a slight smile; granting permission)* Go on then. (MABEL *moves towards archway U.R.)* But don't try and get away. I've found you now and I could easily find you again. Put the car away and then come straight back here.

(MABEL, *baffled and afraid, nods and then hurries out U.R. There is a clap of thunder, much nearer this time. ROBERT walks about the room, his glass in his hand. He comes to the desks, picks up and examines a photograph in a leather frame. He sneers as he looks at the photograph. He puts it down and with a quick glance in the direction of the archway, he dials a number.)*

ROBERT: *(in phone)* Yes, it's me. Oh, yes, I'm in all right. No, not too bad. I've given my elbow more of a clout than I intended. But I'm all right. Yes, I am alone at the moment. But I've got to talk quickly. No, a bit of luck. Her husband's not here. Oh, out somewhere. Now, remember everything we rehearsed. And *don't* leave that phone. She's a much more nervous type than I imagined and . . . . That's all. She's coming. *(He hurriedly rings off, picks up his glass and moves quickly to D.R. MABEL comes into room, doesn't see him immediately, and when she does, gives a little start. They stare at one another for a moment or two. MABEL is anxious, non-plussed. ROBERT'S attitude is that of a man who has the situation well in hand.)*

MABEL: *(at last; moving away a little to L.C.)* Why are you staring at me like that? Please stop it.

ROBERT: I can't. You fascinate me.

MABEL: *(offended)* Really!

ROBERT: A very cool customer, aren't you? But do you sleep

well? Or do you have bad dreams?

MABEL: *(plucks up courage; turning to* ROBERT *with resolution)* Look here! I might owe you something. I admit that.

ROBERT: Oh, you do! No mistake about that.

MABEL: I think the best thing I can do — since we don't want the Police involved — is to give you some money and then you ought to . . . .

ROBERT: Oh, yes! Buy yourself out of your responsibilities! Well, I expected it. People like you always imagine . . . . a bit of position . . . . a little money . . . . and you can opt out of any unpleasantness . . . . no matter who else gets it in the neck. *(He is angry and he crosses to the desk and picks up the photograph in the leather frame)* And I suppose he'd approve. *(He shakes the photograph in her direction.)*

MABEL: *(baffled by this outburst)* Peter?

ROBERT: Keep your mouth shut for the good of the side, eh? Don't let on about your own kind no matter what he's done! Is that what he teahces his snob pupils?

MABEL: But, listen to me . . . .

ROBERT: I wouldn't be at all surprised if it wasn't your husband who talked you into keeping your mouth shut in the first place.

MABEL: That's not my husband.

ROBERT: *(suddenly uncertain)* What?

MABEL: That's my brother-in-law.

ROBERT: *(disconcerted for the first time)* You're . . . . you're not Mrs. Thurlow?

MABEL: No. Whatever made you think I was?

ROBERT: She does live here? This is her house?

MABEL: Yes.

ROBERT: You drove the car in here.

MABEL: Ann's car.

ROBERT: You let yourself in with your key. You seemed to be at home here.

MABEL: I am at home here. I've been staying with my sister for the last couple of weeks.

ROBERT: *(thinks about this for a moment or two, throws the photograph down onto the desk and then sits in the chair behind the desk and laughs quietly)* Your sister! You must think I'm a bit crazy.

MABEL: You did say some strange things. Ask some strange questions.

ROBERT: Yes, I imagine they would sound strange to you. *(Pause)* I made a mistake. I'm sorry.

MABEL: Well, all right. Now, if you wouldn't mind . . . . I think it would be better . . . . if you left now . . . . before my sister gets back.

ROBERT: Where is she?

MABEL: The school is giving a recital in the Town Hall. They've gone to that. She'll be back soon, so if you don't mind . . . . Please.

ROBERT: *(noticing that blood from his elbow has run down his forearm onto his shirt cuff.)* Oh damn! Look at that! *(He feels his elbow through his jacket and winces.)* It's worse that I thought. *(He gets his arm out of the sleeve)* I reckon I'll have to go and get that dressed properly. *(He moves across towards archway U.R.)* But I'll be back.

MABEL: *(alarmed)* Where? Where are you going?

ROBERT: To a doctor — if I can find one at this time. Or the hospital.

MABEL: No. Don't got to a doctor. Clean it up here.

ROBERT: *(surprised by her change of attitude to him)* Very well. Where's the bathroom?

MABEL: In the kitchen'll be all right. It's quicker.

ROBERT: Okay, Miss Nightingale. Lead the way.

  (MABEL goes out into hall, followed by ROBERT. They turn towards kitchen, which is off L. There is another loud rumble of thunder. After a moment or two the front door is heard to close and then ANN comes into the room, taking off and shaking her cape which has got a little wet with the first rain of the thunderstorm. She looks about her, a little surprised to find all the lights on and apparently no one about. She crosses and puts her handbag down on the desk. Turns and walks towards mirror R. and looking in it pats her hair into place.)

ANN: Mabel! *(After a little time she crosses a little up to doorway, and calls again.)* Mabel, where are you?

  (ANN waits for an answer, gets none and returns to desk, shrugging her shoulders. She takes a lipstick from her handbag and remakes her lips, looking into small mirror. At first

she doesn't notice that MABEL *has appeared in the doorway. Then:)*

MABEL: Oh, Ann!

ANN: *(turning towards her)* Whatever's the matter with you? You look as white as a sheet.

MABEL: A terrible thing's happened. *(Swallows hard, preparing to confess)* I took your car.

ANN: You what? Took it? You mean, you drove it?

MABEL: I noticed you'd left the key in after we'd been out shopping this afternoon and well . . . . I had to get a letter off to Gordon. I simply had to, Ann.

ANN: You little fool! If the Police had seen you . . . .

MABEL: I know. I took a chance. I had to let him know that I wanted to go back to him — by first post tomorrow morning. Otherwise he was going to accept that posting to South Africa.

ANN: Oh, Mabel, I've been on to you all day to write that letter. And you had to leave it until . . .

MABEL: I know. I kept putting it off. I didn't know what to say. I didn't want it to look as if I was begging him to take me back.

ANN: You and your pride!

MABEL: When the letter was written I found out that I'd missed the last collection from the box. So I had to go down town — to the General . . . .

ANN: But didn't you realize that if the Police had stopped you for anything . . . . even a parking offence . . . . with that six months' suspended sentence hanging over you . . . .

MABEL: I knew there was a risk but I thought, if I'm careful . . .

ANN: Oh, well, I suppose there 's no harm done if you 're sure no one saw you.

MABEL: No, but . . . .

ANN: Well, thank God for that!

MABEL: But on the way back . . . . just outside he . . . . I . . . . I hit someone.

ANN: Oh, God, no!

MABEL: Not badly. Practically nothing. Just a few scratches, that's all. And it wasn't my fault. He seemed to jump out in front of me. He was hiding behind that big bush at the end of the drive and he jumped out towards me.

ANN: Jumped out . . . ? Oh, come on, Mabel, that's not very

likely, is it?

MABEL: It's true. I think he did it on purpose.

ANN: *(looking at her pityingly)* Where is he now?

MABEL: In the kitchen. (ANN *glances in the direction of the serving-hatch and notices that it is not fully closed.)* His elbow's grazed. He's cleaning it up.

ANN: *(alarmed)* In the kitchen? *(She signifies to MABEL to say no more and quickly crosses up L. and slides the serving-hatch into position.)*

MABEL: *(in a hushed voice)* Don't be angry with me, Ann. Help me.

ANN: One thing we've certainly got to do — and that is to talk this man into keeping quiet about this affair. If he tells the Police, they will investigate . . . . and then you're lost.

MABEL: I know. But I don't think he will tell the police. *(slight pause)* But . . . .

ANN: What?

MABEL: He's been saying some strange things to me.

ANN: Strange things! What do you mean?

MABEL: I couldn't quite understand what he was getting at . . . but . . . er, well, sort of veiled threats.

ANN: Money, you mean! He's asked for money?

MABEL: No. I offered him money but he refused.

ANN: *(impatiently)* Then what do you mean — threats?

ROBERT: *(entering through archway. He smiles, and carries his jacket. The shirt of his injured arm is rolled up. He doesn't see ANN at first — or pretends not to see her.)* It's not too bad. I told you not to worry. Good Lord, I'm not the sort of man who's going to make a fuss about a few scratches. Look, would you be good enough to tie this handkerchief around my elbow?

  (As MABEL does this there is a vivid flash of lightning and a roll of thunder, now much nearer. MABEL shudders at the sound of the thunder.)

MABEL: *(pulling herself together)* Oh, this is my sister, Mrs. Thurlow.

ANN: Good evening. I'm glad you're not too badly injured Mr . . . . Mr . . . .

ROBERT: Thank you, Mrs. Thurlow. My name's Wrightson. Robert Wrightson. *(He stares at ANN while MABEL continues the dressing of the elbow.)* So you're Mrs. Ann Thurlow.

ANN: *(surprised by his tone)* Why, yes.

ROBERT: It's your husband who's headmaster of the posh grammar school here . . . . what's it called? . . . . Ransome's.

ANN: *(vaguely flattered)* You've heard of him?

ROBERT: Oh, yes. Yes, indeed I have. (MABEL *has finished the bandaging.)* Thank you. That's fine. *(He turns back to* ANN) I don't know if your sister told you, Mrs. Thurlow, but at first I mistook her for you.

MABEL: *(startled by a flash of lightning and more thunder)* Oh, I hate thunderstorms.

(The front door is heard to close and a moment later PETER *whose coat is wet with rain, comes in, shaking the wetness from him.)*

PETER: *(as he enters, not noticing* ROBERT *at first)* No bridge tonight. The Barkers aren't coming. Sheila's managed to acquire a migraine.

ANN: *(defending her)* I'm not surprised with this storm about.

PETER: *(seeing* ROBERT) Oh!

ANN: Oh, darling, this is Mr. Wrightson, Mr. Wrightson, my husband.

PETER: How do you do? (PETER *takes note of* ROBERT'S *bandaged elbow as he gingerly slips his arm into his coat's sleeve.)* What's happened? Have you . . . ?

ANN: Mr. Wrightson had a little accident. Right outside the house. And Mabel brought him in.

PETER: *(ever hospitable)* Yes. Of course.

ROBERT: I was lucky. It's not much, thank goodness.

PETER: You look a bit shaky. Won't you sit down.

ROBERT: Thank you. *(He sits on settee.)*

PETER: *(crosses to desk with his brief-case from which he takes some papers and books and puts them on the desk.)* It wasn't anything to do with those uneven flagstones outside, was it? I can tell you I've been on to the council half-a-dozen times about them. I daresay someone'll have to break his neck before anything's done.

ROBERT: No, it wasn't that.

(There are a few moments of silence. ANN'S *glance to* MABEL *signifies that she has no option but to confess.)*

MABEL: *(swallowing hard, summoning up courage)* I'll have to tell you the truth, Peter. I was coming back from town in Ann's car and I knocked Mr . . . . Mr. Wrightson down.

PETER: *(angry)* You did what? *(He controls his anger.)* I see. *(Another rumble of thunder and the sound of torrential rain.)*

ANN: *(looking out through french windows)* It's absolutely pelting down. Like the tropics.

PETER: It's hot and steamy enough. *(Slight pause)* Is there anyone I can ring for you, Mr. Wrightson?

ROBERT: *(who hasn't thought of anyone making this offer)* Ring . . . . for me?

PETER: Don't you think you ought to let someone know what's happened to you? Your wife, perhaps.

ROBERT: No. No, there's no one.

PETER: Then a friend — someone who could come and pick you up. A bit later, when this storm's eased up, of course.

ROBERT: (bewildered by the suggestion) I don't know. I'm still a bit shaken. I can't remember . . . .

PETER: *(having to accept the situation but none too happy about it.)* Naturally. *(Slight pause)* Well, the best thing you can do is to take things easily for a while.

MABEL: You told me it was something to do with Miss Carstairs. Your being in this road, I mean. You had to visit someone.

PETER: Miss Carstairs? But she . . . . she died a year ago.

ROBERT: Yes.

PETER: As a matter of fact, it was *exactly* a year ago. The corresponding Friday night, anyway.

ROBERT: *(a little sharply)* Why should you remember that?

PETER: Oh, I wouldn't have done. But when I went through the Crescent just now to get the Barkers I noticed that No. 87 was on the market. I mentioned it to Stan and he said it was a year ago tonight that she was murdered. Apropos of how time flies.

ROBERT: I believe the Police charged the wrong man in that case.

PETER: Really! Well, if it wasn't . . . . what was the fellow's name? . . . Sheldon . . . . If it wasn't he, who was it?

ROBERT: I don't know. I only know — for sure — that it wasn't Derek Sheldon. *(This conversation about the accused man has drained* ROBERT *emotionally. He has to make some excuse for his taut, agitated condition. He clasps his head in his hands.)* Oh, my head!

PETER: *(a bit concerned)* Are you all right?

ROBERT: A bit giddy, that's all. *(Pause)* Could I possibly trespass a bit further on your hospitality and be allowed to lie down quietly for a few minutes?

PETER: *(a little put out by this request but acting hospitably)* Yes. Yes, of course. *(To ANN)* The spare bedroom next to Mabel's?

ANN: Yes.

ROBERT: I'm very grateful.

PETER: You show Mr. Wrightson where it is, will you, Mabel?

MABEL: Yes, all right.

ROBERT: I think if I could close my eyes for a few moments I'll be able to collect my thoughts.

(MABEL *goes out into hall, followed by* ROBERT)

ANN: *(after a slight pause)* I'm sorry, darling.

PETER: About your sister's stupidity, you mean?

ANN: It hasn't turned out to be quite the evening we planned, has it?

PETER: You mean because that man's in the house? Well, I suppose in the circumstances we've got to do what we can for him.

ANN: Mabel's convinced herself that he's not going to the Police about it — and I believe she's right.

PETER: I don't see how you can be so sure.

ANN: From the little Mabel's told me I got the impression that he threw himself in front of that car on purpose.

PETER: Good Lord, why should he do that?

ANN: *(after a pause)* Suicide?

PETER: You don't have to *throw* yourself under a car Mabel's driving. Stand anywhere in the road and you'll achieve the same object.

ANN: No, seriously.

PETER: Well, if his intentions were suicidal he didn't make a very good job of it.

ANN: Supposing his courage failed him at the last moment and he pulled back just as the car struck him. Wouldn't that account for the slight injuries he's got?

PETER: I suppose it might.

ANN: And why didn't he want to get in touch with any relatives or friends?

PETER: Perhaps he hasn't got any.

ANN: And perhaps my explanation is correct. Go on, admit it.

PETER: *(looking at her lovingly)* You're far too pretty to be a detective. *(Smiling as she approaches him)* Am I really going to have you to myself soon? *(They embrace.)*

ANN: It looks like it. Mabel took my car because she desperately wanted to get a letter away to Gordon this evening. She's told him she wants to go back to him.

PETER: That couple have to learn to grow up — to stop doubting everything the other does.

ANN: I've been lecturing her about that for a week. This afternoon she made up her mind. *(Slight pause)* And I think Ruth'll be leaving soon, too.

PETER: I've heard that before.

ANN: She's met someone she's really keen on. Twenty years older than she is and a good deal steadier.

PETER: What is he? An animal trainer or a psychiatrist?

ANN: Oh, darling, don't say things like that. He's an estate agent . . . at the moment. He's retiring shortly and going to live in a villa in Spain.

PETER: Where is she, by the way? I haven't seen her since I got in.

ANN: She's gone into Sutton to see Mr. Lambert. She was terribly excited when she left. You see, tonight's the night. At least, she convinced herself it is.

PETER: Tonight's the night! That sounds like romantic fiction.

ANN: I suppose it's romantic. I hope it isn't fiction. You see, she's expecting a proposal of marriage.

PETER: And what better place for it than Sutton!

ANN: You've been very patient with her Peter. I *am* grateful.

PETER: Both your sisters seem to have a penchant for complicating their lives.

ANN: They haven't been as lucky as I.

PETER: No?

ANN: No. I married you.

PETER: *(lightly)* Don't flatter me, darling. I don't really need it.

ANN: No, you really have been very kind to both of them. And especially Ruth. She's so . . . so . . .

PETER: *(helping her out)* So scatter-brained?

ANN: *(smiling)* I was going to say volatile. Anyway, you've been a darling.

(She kisses him and then moves to settee where she sits and idly turns the pages of a magazine. PETER sits at desk and arranges some papers.)

PETER: When she first came here . . . you know, after that debacle with that man Batson . . . and she had nowhere to go . . . well, I couldn't very well have my wife's sister walking the streets, could I? *(slight pause)* But I didn't realise then that she'd be staying here for close on eighteen months.

ANN: She's made herself useful. You must admit that.

PETER: I wasn't being petty about Ruth's being here for so long but . . . Well, it will be pleasant to have the house to ourselves once more.

ANN: It may not be so long now, darling. Ruth seems to think they'll be married quite quickly.

PETER: Let's hope she's not disappointed again . . . . for the umpteenth time! About a year ago there was that man Macaulay. She expected him to propose. I remember. Spent a whole week up in Watford with his people — and came back empty-handed.

ANN: Oh, that man was a ladies' hairdresser. They're notoriously unreliable with women. Mr. Lambert is fifty-five, solid and respectable.

PETER: I'm glad to hear it. *(He begins to read some of the papers in front of him.)*

ANN: *(after a pause)* I suppose that conference will be coming up again soon?

PETER: *(looking at her archly)* Do you know I believe you can read my mind. I was just thinking about that.

ANN: Of course, I can read your mind. I'd be at a terrible disadvantage if I couldn't.

PETER: Well, I made a decision this afternoon when we were having tea with the mayor before the concert. You looked too lovely to leave — even for a week. *(Pause)* I'm going to turn it down this year.

ANN: Should you do that? You'll get a black mark from the Governors for being a naughty boy.

PETER: I don't think so. I'm established here now. It was different last year when I went to Brussels. I hadn't been long appointed and it made a good impression. Showed I was keen.

ANN: I saw Sempill this morning, by the way. My last appointment with him. He's declared me sane — officially.

PETER: Don't joke about it.

ANN: I'm not. I'm only pointing out that you could have gone to the conference this year because . . . . things are different now.

PETER: That was an awful time, wasn't it?

ANN: I often wonder how I allowed myself to get in such a state.

PETER: Well, this year I'm giving up a free week in Paris. Now you must admit that that shows I must love you very much.

ANN: *(laughing)* Granted!

(The telephone on the desk rings. PETER answers it.)

PETER: *(on phone)* Yes. Peter Thurlow speaking. Who? Chief Inspector Hardy. Yes. When did this happen? All right. I'll come down straight away. Yes, in about five minutes. Goodbye. *(He rings off)*

ANN: *(a little apprehensively)* What is it?

PETER: I've got to go out. Oh, damn it!

ANN: *(rising)* What! Now?

PETER: At once. There's been a break-in at the school.

ANN: Oh, no!

PETER: That was the Police. They want me to check what's missing.

ANN: Well, wait until the rain eases off.

PETER: No. I'll get it over with. I didn't put the car away. It's just outside.

ANN: Don't be too long, darling.

PETER: I won't. I don't suppose the Police can do much tonight, anyway. *(They go together towards the hall. He kisses her. She watches as he opens the front door and goes out. She comes back into the room and crosses to french windows, and stands watching the rain beating against the glass. There is a vivid flash of lightning. MABEL comes in.)*

MABEL: Did I hear Peter go out?

ANN: Yes. There's been some trouble at the school. He had to go down to sort it out.

MABEL: Did he say anything . . . ? *(She raises her eyes to upstairs.)*

ANN: That man?

MABEL: Yes.

ANN: No. What did you expect him to say?

MABEL: Well, he can't stay here much longer, can he?

ANN: We can't very well turn him out — in this storm. In any case, don't you think we owe him some consideration?

MABEL: Yes, but . . . Well, you don't know. But before you came home . . . he frightened me.

ANN: Oh, Mabel, your nerves! And you know how very touchy you get whenever there's a thunderstorm about.

MABEL: I don't think this had anything to do with the storm.

ANN: What didn't have anything to do with the storm?

MABEL: Well, for instance, he said that if I told the whole truth the young man who was convicted of Miss Carstairs' murder would be saved. I didn't know what he was getting at.

ANN: *(with a short, nervous laugh)* I don't suppose you did.

MABEL: Don't you see, Ann? He really thought I had some knowledge — about something that happened a year ago — affecting that case.

ANN: That's ridiculous. You weren't here a year ago.

MABEL: No, but . . . And this is what really frightens me. After a while he realised he'd made a mistake. It wasn't me he intended to question.

ANN: There you are, then.

MABEL: It was you.

ANN: Me? *(pause)* Haven't you somehow got hold of the wrong end of the stick?

MABEL: He said that he knew everything that went on in this house. He'd been told by someone.

ANN: Oh, Mabel, you are making a fuss! Peter's a public figure in the district now. Dozens and dozens of people come here. There's nothing secret about our lives. I daresay half the town knows. *(Pause)* Look here, you happen to knock a man down. And you claim that that very man has some nefarious scheme hatching concerning me. It's a bit too much of a coincidence, isn't it?

MABEL: I keep on thinking about the way he got in front of the car. Well, not really in front, for it was only the side which hit him.

ANN: Well?

MABEL: Oh, it's silly I know but supposing he *used* that accident to get into the house.

ANN: What are you saying?

MABEL: The more I think about it the more convinced I am. *(Slight pause)* He thought *you'd* be driving that car.

ANN: *(after some thought)* It's rather an involved way of coming here to ask questions, isn't it?

MABEL: Perhaps not. If he knew you'd refuse to see him if he came in the normal way.

ANN: *(thinks hard; then smiles)* Of course, there is a more rational explanation. *(Slight pause)* You knocked the poor man down and in your mind you've got to justify yourself. Aren't you trying all the time to convince yourself that it wasn't your fault?

MABEL: *(after considering this; a little reluctant to give in)* Well, yes, you may be right. *(Lightning and thunder, almost simultaneous, frighten MABEL)* Oh, dear, its getting worse and worse.

ANN: You do get in such a state.

MABEL: I'm sorry. I can't help it. *(Slight pause)* Do you mind if I have a drink?

ANN: Help yourself.

MABEL: *(goes to drinks trolley and pours herself a large Scotch)* I'll take it to my room. I'm trying to get interested in a play on the radio . . . . to shut out the storm.

ANN: It'll be over soon. Good-night.

MABEL: I know you think I'm a silly fool — always worrying about nothing. *(Pause. ANN smiles at her but says nothing.)* Well, goodnight, Ann.

(She goes out into hall and upstairs. ANN tries to settle down with her magazine but MABEL'S talk has upset her somewhat. She listens for sounds in the house. But for what, exactly? Footsteps on the stairs, perhaps? The ringing of the telephone makes her jump. She recovers her composure, smiles and crosses to answer the telephone.)

ANN: *(in phone)* Mrs. Thurlow. Yes, that's right. Can you speak to whom? Yes. Yes, he is here. But who's speaking? And how did you know he was here? No, I won't get him. Not until you tell me who you are. *(The caller rings off.* ANN, *mystified, looks at the receiver and then hangs up. She turns and sees* ROBERT *standing in the archway. She is startled.)*

ROBERT: *(kindly)* I didn't mean to alarm you.

ANN: *(with a wry smile)* It's all right, I . . . *(pause)* Wrong numbers can be very disconcerting, can't they? Thieves try this out, you know, to find out if a house is occupied or not.

ROBERT: That was a wrong number, was it?

ANN: Yes. Well, how are you feeling? You look a bit brighter.

ROBERT: I feel better. A bit clearer in the head, thank goodness. But . . . . do you mind if I sit here for a while. (ANN *looks doubtful)*. . . just until the rain stops. *(Taking her consent for granted he sits, settee.)*

ANN: All right. *(Pause)* Would you care for a dink?

ROBERT: No. I don't think so, thanks.

ANN: Now, I won't beat about the bush, Mr. Wrightson. I realise you must have heard some of the conversation between my sister and me earlier . . . . when you were in the kitchen. *(She rises and walks behind him to D.R.)* I'm sorry you've been hurt, of course, and I'd like to satisfy myself that you're all right. But I'm going to ask you not to report that accident.

ROBERT: I told you. I don't intend to make any fuss about it at all.

ANN: Good! *(She crosses to drinks trolley and pours herself a drink.)* Exactly why don't you intend to report that accident to the Police, Mr. Wrightson?

ROBERT: *(slightly uncomfortable and a bit baffled by the line of questioning)* Well . . . . It's not worth causing trouble about.

ANN: Trouble? For whom?

ROBERT: I don't quite understand.

ANN: I think you do. Right from the beginning you've never intended to say anything about it.

ROBERT: What makes you say that?

ANN: My sister was right. You . . . contrived that accident to get into this house. *(She looks steadily at* ROBERT *but he does not answer).* That wasn't a wrong number just now. I said it was to give myself time to think. It was someone asking for you — someone who knew you'd be here. So I think you'd better put your cards on the table. What are you doing in my house, Mr. Wrightson? And I tell you straight, if I am not satisfied with your explanation I shall call in the Police.

ROBERT: And send your sister to prison for six months!

ANN: I've thought about that. *(Slight pause)* I could say I was driving.

ROBERT: *(after thinking about this for a moment or two)* Oh, no, I don't think you'd do that. The wife of a prominent local figure . . . tell lies to the Police. Oh, no! They'd soon find out the truth, anyway.

ANN: *(coolly)* I'm still waiting for your explanation.

ROBERT: Is your husband in the house?

ANN: No. He had to go out. But he'll be back soon.

ROBERT: You've got more spirit than your sister. I'm not surprised. I somehow didn't think she quite filled the bill.

ANN: Don't talk in riddles. What are you doing here?

ROBERT: *(after a thoughtful pause)* You're right, of course. I did fix that accident to get in here.

ANN: Yes?

ROBERT: I knew that if I wrote you wouldn't answer and if I called you'd turn me away. So I had to find some way of getting in here and staying for a while.

ANN: Well, you've done that. So what now?

ROBERT: A little memory test! I want you to cast your mind back to the week at the beginning of October last year when your husband attended an UNESCO conference in Brussels.

ANN: How did you know he . . . ? Oh, of course, it was in the papers.

ROBERT: On the Friday night of that week Miss Carstairs was murdered. You remember we were talking about it earlier.

ANN: Are you, by any chance, a relative of Miss Carstairs?

ROBERT: Not of her, no. *(Pause)* Now, Mrs. Thurlow, that week when your husband was in Brussels.

ANN: Are you suggesting that I might have seen something? You know, someone in the road . . . . acting suspiciously . . . or . . .

ROBERT: The Friday night, Mrs. Thurlow. Where were you on the Friday night?

ANN: A Friday night a year ago! How do you expect me to

remember? I don't remember much about that period, anyway. I wasn't very well.

ROBERT: You seem very self-possessed now, if I may say so.

ANN: Yes, but then . . . .

ROBERT: Then you were highly-strung, excitable . . . .

ANN: Well, I . . . . What are you getting at?

ROBERT: That young man who was arrested for Miss Carstairs' murder. (He rises, crosses D.R. ANN is L.C.) Well, quite frankly he was a bit of a waster, a disappointment to his father. But he certainly wasn't a murderer.

ANN: There must have been enough evidence against him.

ROBERT: Well, he certainly had a motive. He needed money quickly. He owed a bookmaker two hundred pounds.

ANN: Oh!

ROBERT: Then there was that cleaner woman who saw him cross from the entrance to Miss Carstairs' drive at six in the morning and get into the car parked opposite. She remembered the number of the car — said it described her, a hot forty-two — HOT 42. It wasn't difficult for the Police to trace its owner.

ANN: I don't know much about this subject, Mr. Wrightson, but I must say there seems ample evidence to me.

ROBERT: Oh, yes, and there was a lot more besides . . . . the bracelet found in the pocket of his raincoat. His denial to the Police that he'd ever been in the district — made, of course, before he was aware that they could prove he had been.

ANN: Well?

ROBERT: But there was one glaring discrepancy. The autopsy showed that Miss Carstairs died between midnight and one o'clock. But Derek Sheldon didn't drive away until six in the morning. Of course, the Police claimed that he'd been in the house all that time searching for the money. *(Pause)* Would you believe it if I told you he was walking along the Crescent at six in the morning and he saw something sparkle in the dead leaves at the end of Miss Carstairs' drive, that he picked it up, saw that it was of no very great value, put it in his pocket nevertheless — and then forgot all about it until the Police found it there.

ANN: It would be rather hard to believe, wouldn't it?

ROBERT: The truth so very often is, Mrs. Thurlow.

ANN: You know a very great deal about this case, Mr. Wrightson.

ROBERT: I know everything. *(Pause)* Derek Sheldon is my son.

ANN: *(thinking slowly)* I see.

ROBERT: I'm sorry for the deception. I didn't tell you my real name at first. I had to feel my way a bit, you see?

ANN: No, I don't see. *(Pause)* Your son was convicted of that crime, Mr. . . . Mr. Sheldon. I'm sorry but there it is. You say he's innocent. Well, I suppose that's understandable.

ROBERT: My son did leave his car in the Crescent but he was visiting someone in *this* road that night.

ANN: Oh! Who?

ROBERT: A married woman — whose husband was away.

ANN: I see.

ROBERT: He was with her from about nine o'clock in the evening until just before six the next morning, first in London and then in her house.

ANN: If that's true, why didn't he tell the Police?

ROBERT: Because he didn't want his wife to know where he'd been.

ANN: His wife?

ROBERT: Oh, yes, he was married. She was in hospital for a minor op. He'd visited her earlier in the evening. He told the Police this and said that afterwards he'd gone straight home because he was feeling unwell himself.

ANN: Is it any wonder the case looked black against him?

ROBERT: It looked even blacker when they found that bracelet. And when the cleaner picked him out at an identification parade the Police decided they had enough to charge him. Being an old hand he knew that once the Police charge you you don't open your mouth any more.

ANN: Surely you're not going to tell me that he had a perfect alibi and said nothing about it.

ROBERT: As soon a she got a solicitor he told him everything. But telling the truth and proving it are two different things.

ANN: How's that?

ROBERT: Derek knew the woman's Christian name and that her husband and a sister who lived with her were away. Not much else.

ANN: Didn't he know where the house was?

ROBERT: The woman didn't want him driving up to the house

or parking anywhere near — the neighbours might notice. So she got him to pull up in the Crescent and they walked from there.

ANN: Did they go far?

ROBERT: He was never sure. She didn't take him directly. They went through several side roads . . . and came into the house by the back way.

ANN: And it was misty that night.

ROBERT: *(quickly)* How do you know that?

ANN: *(surprised by his sharpness)* Oh, I don't know. I suppose that at some time I've heard it said that on the night of that murder it was misty. That's all. Or I might have read it.

ROBERT: *(after a pause during which he searches her face intently)* Well, you're right. It was pretty thick, And, of course, he'd had a few drinks and he had no reason to think he'd ever be coming to the house again, and therefore he took no pains to identify it.

ANN: What about in the morning?

ROBERT: He left in a hurry. It was scarcely light and it was more misty than ever. He came out by the front door, turned right instead of left and was soon lost. He asked an early morning worker where the Crescent was. He was half a mile adrift.

ANN: So he had no idea where the house was?

ROBERT: It could have been anywhere in any direction within about a quarter of a mile from where he left his car. Of course, at the time he couldn't have cared less. But when he *had* to find the house . . . . well, a pretty hopeless task to pick out one particular house in a heavily built-up area where all the side roads look alike.

ANN: But surely his solicitors tried?

ROBERT: Frankly, I don't think they ever believed his story. But, yes, they tried. Went through the motions, anyway. They made some enquiries but they didn't find anyone, anywhere in the district, who could help. So the story wasn't told in court . . . . and Derek was convicted.

ANN: But somewhere there must have been a woman who knew . . . .

ROBERT: Yes, and still knows. Ever since he was accused of the murder Derek has held on to the hope that that woman would come forward and clear him. But she never has. *(Approaching* ANN *L.C.)* Let's give her the benefit of the doubt and say she was ill at the time and didn't know.

ANN: *(alarmed)* What are you getting at, Mr. Sheldon?

ROBERT: I've visited my son in prison at every opportunity and gradually I've got out of him the whole story, piecing it together bit by bit. Now I can do what he never could. I can prove that alibi.

ANN: Then go straight to the Police. Or tell this solicitor. Let him handle it.

ROBERT: Mrs. Thurlow, I can't help admiring your coolness. Or is it brutal coldness?

ANN: *(offended)* Please don't take that tone with me. I've allowed you a great deal of latitude because I sympathise with your predicament but . . . .

ROBERT: *(roughly)* Now you listen to me. We've got to settle this problem between us. I can see how awful it's going to be for you to have to stand up in public and tell the truth about that night . . . .

ANN: What are you talking about?

ROBERT: I'd like to spare you. But I have no choice.

ANN: Spare me? What do you mean?

ROBERT: You know very well why Derek Sheldon couldn't have killed Miss Carstairs.

ANN: I do? I'm . . . .

ROBERT: Because at the time of the murder he was here, in this house, with you . . . . in your bed.

ANN: You must be mad.

ROBERT: Oh, no.

ANN: Or made some ghastly mistake.

ROBERT: *(showing her a photograph from a newspaper)* Know who that is?

ANN: Of course. It's my husband. That picture was printed in the newspapers.

ROBERT: That's where Derek saw it — in a newspaper, in prison. For the second time! The first time was in your bedroom — in a thin silver frame on your dressing-table.

ANN: No, it can't . . . .

ROBERT: This picture is there, isn't it?

ANN: Yes, but how could anyone . . . . ?

ROBERT: My other son, Frank, came down here pretending to be a journalist and interviewed your husband about his career in this room. He took away with him a mental picture of everything here. It tallied exactly with what Derek remembered.

ANN: *(confused)* A year ago! You've surprised me . . . . I don't . . . .

ROBERT: Oh, I know you weren't yourself at the time. Your nerves were in tatters and that night you were a little tipsy, too.

ANN: No. Not me.

ROBERT: Your husband had gone off to Brussels against your wishes and you . . . . well, you didn't care what happened, did you?

ANN: *(making an attept to go)* You're raving.

ROBERT: *(catching hold of her wrist and restraining her)* Mrs. Thurlow, think about it. I wouldn't say these things to you unless I could prove them, would I?

ANN: *(wrenching herself free)* Then go to the Police, damn you. And I'll sue you for everything you've got.

ROBERT: I'm not going to the Police.

ANN: Ah!

ROBERT: It wouldn't be any good . . . not yet.

ANN: *(recovering her composure somewhat as she realises that there is more bluff to ROBERT than she has been thinking)* You must think I'm crazy. It's obvious what's happened. Your son, in desperation, has *made up* this ridiculous story — though why he should pick on me I don't know . . . . and now you're trying to rough ride your way . . . .

ROBERT: Oh, come off it, Mrs. Thurlow.

ANN: If it were not so outrageous I'd be very angry with you, Mr. Sheldon. As it is I think the best thing for both of us is to forget every word of this conversation. *(Slight pause)* And now, if you're feeling better I think it would be as well if you left this house before Peter gets back.

ROBERT: *(goes D.R. and sits)* I don't intend to leave — until I've got what I came for. That sentence hanging over your sister's head was a bit of luck for me. My insurance! Think very carefully before you kick me out.

ANN: If you repeat your horrible story about me I shall have to defend myself. If that means getting the Police in on this . . . very well, Mabel will have to take her chance. Don't think you can shelter behind her for much longer, Mr. Sheldon.

ROBERT: *(as he sees* ANN *crossing to desk)* What are you going to do?

ANN: *(dialling telephone)* I'm ringing the school to ask Peter to come home at once.

ROBERT: *(in a quiet but menacing voice)* You've got green wallpaper in your bedroom now, Mrs. Thurlow. (ANN *gives him a surprised look. She makes a mistake with the dialling and has to start again.)* The door was open. I noticed when I passed just now. A year ago it was pink, wasn't it?

(ANN *stops dialling and slowly replaces receiver.)*

ANN: *(bewildered; slowly)* How did you know that?

ROBERT: I told you I could prove my story. You didn't seem to believe me. *(He rises and goes to drinks trolley.)* I think I'll have that drink you offered me now. *(He pours a drink, Pause.)* And then you can talk.

ANN: *(after staring at him wide-eyed for a moment or two.)* No. I'm not saying anything. No. *(A look of horror comes onto her face and she runs from the room.* ROBERT *walks slowly to entrance of hall and looks upstairs. There is a loud rumble of thunder. He crosses to telephone and dials a number.)*

ROBERT: *(in phone)* Hello, Frank. So far, so good. Yes, I'll be able to stay the night. There's a colossal storm going on down here and no one's going to kick a sick man out into the street. *(Slight laugh)* Oh, yes, no doubt about it. You should have seen the panic in her eyes just a few moments ago. No, she hasn't admitted anything yet. She's got a lot to lose. And she's as tough and cool as they come. But she'll tell the truth . . . after she's slept on it. *(A short, harsh laugh)* That is, if she does sleep. And I shall be having another go at her in the morning.

CURTAIN

A NIGHT IN OCTOBER

ACT ONE
SCENE TWO

THE SCENE *is the same. It is about breakfast − time the following morning.* RUTH *crosses from R.C. to french windows and opens them and stands for a moment breathing in the fresh, cool air of the sunny morning which has followed the storm. After a few moments she turns D.L. and, taking a duster from the pocket of her apron, begins to flick lightly over the desk. She picks up the photograph of* PETER *in the leather frame and gazes at it with admiraion. She hears* ANN *enter U.R. and replaces it a little guiltily − and hurriedly, and turns smiling to* ANN.

RUTH: You can ring the bells. It's happened.
ANN: He proposed?
RUTH: Men are so obvious. I knew what was on his mind the last time we met.
ANN: And it was still on his mind last night?
RUTH: Well, he got it off his mind last night. You'll soon be rid of me. Special licence next Wednesday week.
ANN: *(crosses to C. at the same time as* RUTH. *They meet and embrace, a little formally)* Oh, Ruth, I'm so happy for you!
RUTH: Of course, he's a good bit older than I am.
ANN: That's not always a bad thing.
RUTH: I've never had much luck with the younger ones.
ANN: You'll settle down now and be very happy, I'm sure.
RUTH: *(turning away a little to L.C.)* I shan't like leaving here. I shall miss you and Peter.

ANN: I think it's time you left.

RUTH: *(swinging around)* What!

ANN: I meant for your own good. When you came here after you broke up with that Batson man we thought you'd be staying perhaps a week or two. You've been here — what is it now? — fifteen, sixteen months.

RUTH: *(hurt)* I'm sorry. I didn't realise you resented it.

ANN: Oh, Ruth, don't be so touchy. I don't resent it. I'm thinking of you. You're my sister and you've become a sort of house-keeper here. Don't you see that you owe it to yourself to break away?

RUTH: I've been very happy. And I've never complained. *(Pause)* But you're right. I have to break away. But I can't forget how kind you and Peter have been to me. Especially Peter.

ANN: *(with a little smile)* Oh! Why especially Peter?

RUTH: You're my own family. But Peter . . . . *(her expression betrays her admiration)* . . . . yet he's always been nice to me. *(With a little laugh)* It's a wonder he didn't get fed up long ago, this house becoming a rest-home for the Maxby sisters.

ANN: He's a very kind man. And I'm sure he's very fond of you, Ruth.

RUTH: He *is* a kind man. I hope you realise how lucky you are, Ann.

ANN: I do. No doubt about that.

RUTH: Both Mabel and I have made a mess of things so far as men are concerned. But you . . . .

ANN: You're going to be all right from now on. You'll see.

RUTH: *(after a pause)* Where *is* Peter? I haven't seen him this morning.

ANN: It's Saturday, Ruth. He's still in bed.

RUTH: *(looking at* ANN *anxiously)* Are you all right?

ANN: Of course. *(Having to make an excuse for her rather jaded appearance)* I was thinking about the house . . . . how quiet it's going to be. Mabel is going, too, you know. Gordon is coming for her, later today, I expect.

RUTH: They've made it up?

ANN: For the tenth and last time, I understand. And you'll be away after next week.

RUTH: *(still concerned)* Are you sure you're all right?

ANN: Why do you ask?

RUTH: When I got in last night, bursting with my news, I had no one to tell it to.

ANN: There was a break-in at the school. Peter had to go down and see what was missing. And I went to bed just after ten.

RUTH: Very unlike you to be so early. You told me once that you never slept if you went to bed before midnight.

ANN: I was right. I didn't sleep much.

RUTH: There you are, you see.

ANN: Ruth, I want to ask you something.

RUTH: Yes?

ANN: You remember — about a year ago — when I had that breakdown.

RUTH: You're not feeling like that again?

ANN: You know I'm not.

RUTH: Well?

ANN: You remember Peter went to Brussels to that UNESCO conference.

RUTH: *(pause)* Yes. What about it?

ANN: When he came back he got that specialist, Sempill, in . . . and I was on that treatment . . . you know, the drugs and things. Well, you're going to think this very silly but . . . do you know I'm not absolutely certain of everything that happened about that time.

RUTH: No wonder, I suppose.

ANN: Some things are real enough, vivid and clear . . . . but others . . . . like in a dream . . . . a nightmare, really.

RUTH: Are you speaking especially of that week when Peter was away?

ANN: Yes.

RUTH: Well, Mabel can help you more about that week than I can.

ANN: Oh?

RUTH: You spent that week with her. Surely you remember that?

ANN: Yes, that was the arrangement, wasn't it?

RUTH: Peter didn't want you left alone in the house. And I was going up to Watford for the week . . . . to Tom Macaulay and his people. And what a fiasco that was, too!

ANN: Yes, I remember that. It didn't work out as you'd imagined.

RUTH: You can say that again! His parents took one look at me and decided that their son must be under the influence of drugs . . . . or gone berserk or something . . . . to want to marry me.

ANN: Oh, Ruth!

RUTH: It's true. I might have been a leper . . . . with a ring through my nose, too . . . . the way they looked at me. And as for Tom . . . . He wavered between kowtowing to them and getting me into bed. It was the most humiliating few days I've ever spent.

ANN: No more of that sort of thing, Ruth.

RUTH: *(after a pause)* Now, what is it that's troubling you about that week?

ANN: I wish I could be sure what happened, that's all.

RUTH: I told you. You went to Mabel's. After we'd said 'Goodbye' to Peter you ran me into the station in your car. And you were to go straight on to Mabel's.

ANN: *(doubtfully)* Yes, that's right.

RUTH: I got back here *(slight hesitation as she recollects dates and times)* on the next Saturday afternoon — just after you.

ANN: That's all you know, then?

RUTH: You did say you'd been working hard during the week on that novel you were writing.

ANN: Oh, that! Yes, I finished that.

RUTH: But why has all this come up now? What does it matter what happened a year ago?

ANN: Perhaps it doesn't matter at all.

RUTH: Shall I get you some coffee?

ANN: *(crossing to french window)* A little later, perhaps. I'm going for a walk.

RUTH: Where?

ANN: Just for a stroll. Get some air. It smells so fresh and clean after the storm. I might walk down to the village and back. (ANN *goes out through french windows and* RUTH *watches her rather anxiously. Then she continues with her dusting and once again picks up the photo of* PETER *and looks at it lovingly. She takes it a little nearer to the windows to get more light on it and then hears* PETER *coming down the stairs. She replaces it hurriedly on the desk as he enters. He is wearing a dressing-gown over shirt and trousers.)*

PETER: Hello, Ruth. Where's Ann?

RUTH: Ann? She's gone for a walk.

PETER: Oh! *(He crosses to desk with morning mail and sits)* Did she tell you about the trouble at the school last night?

RUTH: Yes.

PETER: I think the Police have got a good idea who they're looking for.

RUTH: Was there a lot stolen?

PETER: Three or four microscopes from the biology lab. and a couple of dozen silver medals which we kept in a glass-fronted case in the gym. *(Pause)* And how did you get on last night?

RUTH: *(in a less excited tone than one would expect)* We're being married on Wednesday week.

PETER: Oh, that's great. *(He rises and goes to her at C.)* Congratulations. I'm so pleased for you.
(He gives her a little kiss. She tries to make the kiss last longer than he intended. He breaks away U.L.)

RUTH: I shall be sorry to leave here, Peter.

PETER: Ann'll miss you. You can be sure of that. *(He sits at desk)*

RUTH: And you?

PETER: Eh?

RUTH: I expect you'll miss me a little bit, too. *(She laughs to cover the directness of this assessment of her relationship with him.)*

PETER: *(joking, lightly)* Yes, of course. A little bit.

RUTH: I know I've been here a long time . . . . I must have outstayed my welcome . . . . but I've tried to . . . . to please you.

PETER: Yes, you have. *(To please her)* I shall miss you, Ruth. Truly.

RUTH: *(satisfied, she smiles, then, after a slight pause)* Shall I get some breakfast for you?

PETER: Has Ann had anything?

RUTH: Not yet.

PETER: Then I'll wait for her. *(He gets up and crosses to drinks cabinet)* We've got some grapefruit crush here. That'll do nicely for the time being. *(He pours himself a drink and picking up the newspapers from a low table R.C. returns to his desk and sits.)*

RUTH: *(as she is dusting mantelpiece on R. side of room)* She doesn't seem all that well again.

PETER: *(looking up from newspaper)* Eh?

RUTH: Surely you've noticed.

PETER: Who? Ann? I certainly haven't. Yesterday she seemed on top of the world.

RUTH: Was she asleep when you got in last night?

PETER: *(thinking about it for a moment)* Yes. Sound asleep.

RUTH: Or pretending to be.

PETER: *(not too pleased)* Whatever makes you say that?

RUTH: You haven't seen her this morning, have you?

PETER: No. You know I haven't.

RUTH: I have. I swear she hasn't slept a wink.

PETER: *(after some thought)* Perhaps she was up early. She might be tired, that's all. There's nothing at all wrong with her these days, thank God.
(As if to dismiss the whole matter he returns to the reading of his newspaper.)

RUTH: Oh, well, let's hope you're right. But . . . . *(crossing towards him)* . . . . I don't want to be an alarmist, Peter, but this morning she's been talking in . . . . a strange way.

PETER: *(getting annoyed with RUTH)* Talking about what, for God's sake?

RUTH: About what happened a year ago . . . . when you were in Brussels. She doesn't seem to be able to remember what she did that week.

PETER: *(after considering this for a moment or two)* Oh, what the hell does it matter anyway, Ruth?

RUTH: That's what I told her.

PETER: If I remember rightly she spent that week with Mabel over at Abinger. Yes, that's right. I fixed it up with her before I left here because I didn't want to leave Ann alone in the house.

MABEL: *(entering)* Did I hear my name being bandied about?

PETER: Hello, Mabel. We were just talking about that week Ann spent with you — what is it? — about a year ago now . . . When I had to go over to Brussels.

MABEL: Oh!

PETER: *(who would like to drop the subject; with an attempt at humour)* All I can say is you couldn't have made it very exciting for her. Or perhaps you laced the tea with brandy and spent the week in alcoholic fog.

MABEL: She wasn't very well at that time. She didn't seem to notice what was going on.

PETER: She did quite a few silly things about that time, I remember. There was that silver cigarette box she gave me on our third wedding anniversary. After I gave up smoking she had it on her dressing-table. She used to keep hair clips in it.

RUTH: I've searched the house over and over again.

PETER: Not the sort of thing you'd mislay and yet . . . . Poor Ann hasn't the slightest idea what she did with it. *(Pause)* After all, it is a year ago. What do you remember about that week, Mabel? Not much, I should imagine.

MABEL: No. It was a quiet week. We didn't go out much.

PETER: *(with a little laugh)* Well, perhaps that's why she can't remember, Ruth. An uneventful week! A year ago! Who could?

RUTH: *(summing it up, as it were)* I suppose it's always a worry to her.

PETER: What?

RUTH: That she should have that . . . . that nervous trouble again.

PETER: *(angry)* That's nonsense, Ruth. And you know it is. She's perfectly all right these days.

MABEL: *(after an awkward pause)* I'm going to get myself some breakfast.

RUTH: *(to* PETER*)* Sure I can't get you . . . . some coffee, at least?

PETER: All right, then. But nothing to eat until Ann gets back.

RUTH: Okay. *(Taking* MABEL'S *arm, piloting her out)* Wednesday week.

MABEL: What?

RUTH: My wedding, of course.

MABEL: Oh! I'm so pleased.

(They have been talking as they go out. PETER *sits for a while, staring out through the french windows. Finally he dismisses his worst fears with a shrug and a little laugh and returns to reading his newspaper.* ROBERT *comes downstairs and into the room.)*

ROBERT: *(a little diffidently)* Good morning, Mr. Thurlow.

PETER: *(looking up, surprised)* Oh! Good morning. Pardon me. I didn't realise . . . .

ROBERT: That I was still here? Your wife didn't have the heart to turn me out into that storm last night.

PETER: No. Of course not.

ROBERT: Have you spoken to her this morning?

PETER: *(puzzled by the question)* Spoken to her? No, as a matter of fact, I haven't seen her.

ROBERT: Ah!

PETER: Would you like some coffee?

ROBERT: Thank you. That would be very nice.

PETER: *(going to serving-hatch, sliding it open a little)* Make it two cups, Ruth, please.

RUTH: *(off, in kitchen)* Is Ann back already, then?

PETER: No. I have . . . . a guest. *(He closes the hatch.)* Sit down Mr. . . . . Mr. Wrightson.

ROBERT: *(sitting on settee C.)* Thanks.

PETER: *(at his desk; after a pause)* Why did you ask me if I'd spoken to my wife this morning?

ROBERT: *(a little nonplussed for the moment but recovering quickly)* I wondered if she'd mentioned why I'm here. What I was doing in this road last night.

PETER: You told her, did you? When I was down at the school?

ROBERT: Yes.

PETER: Do you want to tell me?

ROBERT: I intended to. *(Slight pause)* On second thoughts it would be better for me if I got my chief to have a few words with you.

PETER: *(puzzled)* Your chief?

ROBERT: At the Home Office. *(Very pleasantly)* Do you mind if I use your phone?

PETER: Go ahead.

(PETER *gets up from his chair at the desk and moves away towards french windows.* ROBERT *rises and crosses to phone and dials a number.)*

ROBERT: *(in phone)* I hope I can get through quickly. It's a bit of a problem sometimes — especially on Saturday mornings. There's only a relief on the switchboard. *(But he does get through)* Oh, hello! Revision section, please. Mr. Haines' office. Thanks. *(He waits)* Mr. Haines? Wrightson here, sir. Good morning. I've got Mr. Thurlow with me now. Would you have a few words with him? No, no. No problem. I think he'd appreciate it, sir. *(Slight pause)* Yes, we are alone at the moment. Thank you, sir. *(He proffers the phone to* PETER *who moves to take it.* ROBERT *withdraws to R.C.)*

PETER: *(in phone)* Peter Thurlow here. *(He listens)* Naturally I'll do what I can to co-operate. Just one thing. How long is this investigation likely to continue? Oh, well, that's all right then. Goodbye. *(He rings off)*

ROBERT: *(after a pause)* He's put you in the picture, I hope.

PETER: Yes. Well, I suppose we all have a duty to help to rectify a miscarriage of justice.

ROBERT: I'm glad you see it like that, Mr. Thurlow.

PETER: And you think there's someone living in this road who'll be able to help you?

ROBERT: Exactly.

PETER: I shouldn't think it would be easy for you.

ROBERT: No?

PETER: After all, a year ago. Who knows? Who remembers?

ROBERT: The person I'm after remembers all right.

PETER: Ah, here's our coffee.

(RUTH *brings in two cups of coffee on a small tray. She puts the tray down on low table near the settee and then takes one of the cups to* PETER *at the desk.)* This is Mr. Wrightson, Ruth. He'll be staying here for a little while . . . the rest of the day, maybe.

RUTH: *(nods to* ROBERT, *then turns to* PETER) I'm going to start collecting my things together, Peter. Upstairs. When Ann comes back call out for me and I'll come down and get you something to eat.

PETER: All right, Ruth. I will. *(As* RUTH *goes out* PETER *feels he has to explain her presence in the house.)* Ruth is my wife's other sister. She's been living with us for . . . . just over a year now.

ROBERT: I fancied I saw a family likeness.

PETER: *(surprised at this)* Oh? Yes, I suppose there is. I'd never really noticed.

ROBERT: The other sister . . . . is her name, Mabel? . . . . She doesn't live here permanently.

PETER: No. She's married. She lives at Abinger. She's been staying with us just a few days. *(making an excuse)* They're having the place re-decorated.

ROBERT: I see. *(He sips his coffee.)*

PETER: I'm afraid I can't be of much help to you. I wasn't even in the country . . . . not the whole of that week. And no one else in this house is going to be of much use to you, either.

ROBERT: Oh?

PETER: The house was unoccupied . . . . from the Sunday, just after I left — Ruth went up to Watford for the week and my wife was over with her sister in Abinger until . . . . oh, early on the Saturday afternoon, I believe. I think they arrived back at the house at about the same time. I got in about seven that evening. I don't think they'd heard of Miss Carstairs' death until we read about it in a paper I'd brought in with me.

ROBERT: Um! *(sips his coffee)* Did you know her?

PETER: Miss Carstairs? No. I'd heard about her, of course . . . that she'd sold off everything of value in the house — turned it all into cash. She thought it less of a magnet for burglars. Easier to hide notes than antiques and paintings.

ROBERT: The murderer had the floorboards up in the bedroom but it was the Police who found the money. Seven thousand pounds — mostly in ten-pound notes.

PETER: You would know these details. It's your job.

ROBERT: It was ironic that she was killed for practically nothing. All the murderer could lay his hands on were trinkets — cheap jewellery, ear-rings, a necklace, a bracelet. Only the bracelet's been recovered so far. *(Pause)* If you came to burgle a house would you leave your car parked outside?

PETER: I suppose it does rather give the game away.

ROBERT: I think the Police were wrong . . . . to connect the car with the burglary . . . . and the murder.

PETER: What else then? Are you suggesting that the owner of that car was . . . . well, perhaps visiting someone who lives around here?

ROBERT: That's just it. *(Slight pause)* I think I'll take a stroll around to the Crescent and have another look at No. 87. Thanks for the coffee. I'll see you. *(With a slight smile on his face and a casual wave he goes out U.R. The telephone bell rings.)*

PETER: *(answering phone)* Yes. Oh, is that you, Gordon? How are you? Good. Yes, I'll get her. *(Puts handset down on*

desk, crosses to serving hatch and slides it open.) Mabel!
Mabel, it's Gordon.

(Very quickly MABEL *runs from the kitchen, enters U.R. and crosses to phone.)*

MABEL: *(in phone; excitedly)* Hello, Gordon. Yes, darling.
You got my letter, then? Yes, I do want to. Really. Oh, I
know, we just can't go on being silly. We love each other too
much, don't we, darling? *(with a little laugh)* Sometimes you
wouldn't think so. But we do. *(Pause)* This evening? You'll
come down and pick me up? Wonderful, darling. Till then.
Goodbye. *(She blows a kiss into the phone and then hangs
up.)* Oh, Peter, everything's all right.

PETER: I'm very glad.

*(In her excitement she crosses to him, giving him a little
kiss and hugs him. Then she hurries from the room. The
telephone rings.* PETER *crosses to phone and picks it up.
In phone.)* Yes, Peter Thurlow speaking. Oh, yes, Chief Inspector. Well, that was quick work. When would you want
me? Yes, I understand you want to get it cleared up but
. . . . it's a bit awkward at the moment. *(Tetchily)* Oh, very
well, as soon as I can then. Goodbye. *(He rings off.)*

(ANN *enters at french windows)*

PETER: Ah! Hello, darling!

ANN: Hello! What a beautiful morning.

PETER: Yes. Where have you been?

ANN: I *was* going down to the shops. But I didn't get that far.

PETER: Are you all right?

ANN: *(a hint of doubt, of hesitation)* Yes. Yes, of course, I am.
(Pause) Why do you ask?

PETER: Ruth said you looked a bit jaded this morning.

ANN: Ruth did?

PETER: Yes. She said you hadn't had a good night. But you
were sound asleep when I got in.

ANN: Was I?

(PETER *crosses to her at french windows, playing the doctor
in a joking way)*

PETER: *(lifting her face towards his with his fingers under
her chin)* Now, Mrs. Thurlow, let's have a look at you.

ANN: *(joining in the joke)* Yes, doctor.

PETER: *(after a moment or two)* You look pretty good to me.

(He kisses her) But you will tell me .... truthfully — if there's anything worrying you?

ANN: *(a little hesitantly)* There isn't. *(She crosses away to R.C. and notices* ROBERT'S *empty coffee cup on the low table near the settee.)* That man is still here?

PETER: Man? Oh, you mean Mr. Wrightson. He's gone out.

ANN: Gone away, you mean?

PETER: No. Just for a walk.

ANN: Who is he, Peter? And what does he want here?

PETER: I had an idea that somehow he worried you. But there's no need. Really there isn't, darling.

ANN: You've found out who he is, then?

PETER: He's a Mr. Wrightson, an official of the Home Office. He works for the department whose job it is to review prison sentences. There! *(He crosses to* ANN *and gives her a reassuring hug. Then he holds her at arm's length and looks straight into her face.)* I knew you had some queer suspicions about him last night when you told me that you thought he'd tried to commit suicide.

ANN: *(slowly moving away from* PETER) I was wrong about that.

PETER: Of course, you were.

ANN: He contrived that accident to get into the house.

PETER: Oh, Ann, what an idea! Whatever put that into your head?

ANN: He did.

PETER: What?

ANN: He told me so himself .... last night, after you'd gone out.

PETER: *(worried about her, looks at her intently)* No, it's .... you must have misunderstood him.

ANN: That's what he said.

PETER: Then he must have been joking.

ANN: Funny sense of humour!

PETER: And why should he go to the trouble of getting himself knocked about when he could have come here officially?

ANN: *(sharply; convinced she is making a telling point)* Then why didn't he come officially?

PETER: Well, that's cleared up now. I've spoken to his chief on the phone.

ANN: When? Yesterday?

PETER: No. This morning. A few minutes ago.

ANN: *(suspiciously)* You're hiding something from me.

PETER: *(amazed at this suggestion)* Hiding something! Darling, I know no more than you do about this business. I don't particularly like having that man about. But supposing there has been a miscarriage of justice . . . . well, don't you think we ought to do what's in our power to put it right?

ANN: Is that really all there is to it?

PETER: What else could there be?

ANN: When you came back from the Barkers last night and that man was here you didn't seem surprised. And you didn't seem annoyed, either, as I imagined you would be.

PETER: Ann, the poor fellow had just been knocked down by your sister. And there was that tremendous storm going on. What did you expect me to do, kick him out?

ANN: After you'd gone to the school last night he came downstairs, into this room and asked me a lot of questions.

PETER: What sort of questions?

ANN: About what I was doing a year ago — the night Miss Carstairs was killed.

PETER: *(after a slight, thoughtful pause)* Is that so remarkable, Ann? He's down here to find that out from everyone around here.

ANN: Do you know what else he told me . . . . that his name wasn't Wrightson but Sheldon, and he was the father of the man now in prison for the murder?

PETER: *(rather anxious)* Ann . . . . are you sure about that?

ANN: And he knew a great deal about this house . . . . that we used to have pink wallpaper in our bedroom whereas now it is green.

PETER: *(looking at her intently, and a little sadly)* Ann, don't be angry with me for saying this but . . . . haven't you got confused somehow. Haven't you been dreaming . . . . or lying awake for hours imagining things?

ANN: So that's it! You still think there's something wrong with me.

PETER: No. No.

ANN: That man's a doctor, isn't he? A doctor or a psychiatrist!

PETER: *(amazed at this suggestion)* Good Lord, Ann, why

should you think that?

ANN: You brought him into this house, didn't you?

PETER: I did? Really, Ann! Take a grip on yourself.

ANN: To test me.

PETER: *(going to her quickly and taking her into his comforting arms)* That's an outrageous notion, darling. There's absolutely nothing wrong with you now. And there never will be again. All that's over. You know that.

ANN: I thought I did.

PETER: You mustn't doubt it. All those pressures — just after I got the headship — well, they were too much for you. And I didn't help, only thinking of myself, mycareer. We had a rotten patch. But it hasn't been like that since. *(Pause)* I love you, Ann. I would never do anything underhand as you've suggested.

ANN: Promise me!

PETER: Do I have to?

ANN: Yes, please. I need reassurance. I'm sorry but I do.

PETER: I promise.

ANN: *(drawing away from him a little)* Ruth was right. I did have a bad night.

PETER: I should go and lie down now, then. I have to go into town again. The Police rang me up just now. They've dug up some stolen things in a fellow's garden . . . somewhere off the High Street. They've found three microscopes and a box of silver medals. They're bound to be the school's but I've got to identify them officially.

ANN: *(following him as he moves towards doorway U.R.)* Don't be too long.

PETER: *(going into hallway, replaces his dressing-gown with a jacket and re-appears at archway)* One quick look and I'll say, 'Yes, that's ours' and I'll come back at once.

ANN: I hope you don't think I've been too silly.

PETER: *(embracing her)* Why don't you remember that I love you and forget everything else. *(He gives her a little kiss, smiles, she returns the smile a little weakly, and then he goes out. After a moment, ANN crosses to desk, picks up newspaper and glances at it idly. MABEL comes in.)*

MABEL: I've just caught sight of myself in the mirror. *(Pulling at her hair.)* Look at it. I'll have to do something about it.

I may not be Helen of Troy but somehow I've got to acquire a bit of come-hither before tonight.

ANN: Try that little place in the village — Maison Henriques.

MABEL: Maison Henriques! Sounds very posh. But what are they like?

ANN: The main thing is they're handy. Ring up for an appointment

MABEL: No. They might not be able to fit me in. I'll got down and *make* them do it.

ANN: *(with a little smile)* You usually get your way.

MABEL: In the end, yes. *(she moves towards the doorway U.R.)* I could always buy a wig. Platinum blonde, I think!

ANN: *(checking MABEL as she goes out)* Oh, Mabel!

MABEL: *(turning)* Yes?

ANN: About that time I was supposed to come over to you for the week.

MABEL: What?

ANN: When Peter went to that conference in Brussels and Ruth was in Watford. Remember? A year ago.

MABEL: Oh, yes?

ANN: I came, you know.

MABEL: *(shaking her head, slowly)* Oh, Ann, you know very well you didn't.

ANN: I did. I couldn't make myself heard at the front door so I went round to the back, to the kitchen door. I was just about to knock when I heard you and Gordon.

MABEL: Oh!

ANN: You were in the middle of the most unholy row.

MABEL: *(with a wry smile)* That wasn't very unusual for Gordon and me.

ANN: I thought it wasn't the best time for me to present myself. So I came back here.

MABEL: *(chastened)* I meant to ring you . . . . and ask what had happened to you and why you hadn't come . . . . but . . . . well, along that time you changed your mind so often and . . . and . . . . well, we were having a lot of trouble then . . . . Gordon and me . . . . and I . . . . I just forgot.

ANN: I didn't mind in a way. I was alone in the house and I had a wonderful chance to work on my novel.

MABEL: Novel?

ANN: I told you about it. A romantic novel. I retyped the last four chapters in four days and then I took it up to London.

MABEL: *(excited)* Don't tell me it's going to be published.

ANN: No, it's not. It never will be.

MABEL: *(disappointed)* Oh!

ANN: I went up to London on the Friday afternoon and stayed overnight. I delivered my typescript to a publisher's in Bedford Square on the Saturday morning. Then I came home.

MABEL: Did they say anything nice about your book?

ANN: They said what was probably the best thing for me. They said they didn't want to publish it. I didn't want Peter to know. He was always rather superior about my literary efforts. And I still don't want him to know. And I don't want him to know that I spent a night alone in London when he was away. Do you follow me?

MABEL: *(rather thrilled by the idea)* You want me to tell a little white lie?

ANN: If he . . . . or anyone else . . . . should ask you about that week say that I was with you the whole time. You can be vague about it. After all, it was a year ago.

MABEL: Rely on me. Any woman who's been married for seven years knows how to play the diplomat.

ANN: It's just that it'll been less recrimination, less worry for everyone that way.

MABEL: Sure. I understand. You'll probably have to do the same for me at some time. *(She winks at* ANN*)* Oh, I shouldn't say that, should I? Everything's all right now. God's in his heaven and . . . all that!

ANN: *(with a smile)* Go on. Go and get your hair done.

MABEL: Okay. *(Pulling at her hair)* Monsieur Henriques you are about to face your supreme test. *(She goes out U.R. ANN picks up newspaper and sits at desk. Her eyes rise from the page and alight on the telephone. She is thoughtful and worried. She gets up, goes to bookcase and takes Telephone Directory from top shelf. She returns to the desk and searches for a number. She finds it and, after a slight hesitation, dials it)*

ANN: *(In phone)* Home Office? Would you please put me through to the department that deals with the review of prison sentences? *(Pause)* You don't know. Well, is there a Duty Officer? Could I speak to him, then? *(waits)* Oh, hello! My name is Thurlow. I'm the wife of the headmaster of Ransome's

Grammar School at Sutton. Can you help me, please? A man has come to my house. He says his name is Wrightson and he claims to be working for the Home Office. He claims to be reopening the investigation into the murder of a Miss Carstairs who was killed about a year ago . . . . You don't know anything about it? Yes, yes, I do have doubts that he's genuine. Get in touch with the Police. No, I haven't done yet. Yes, I see. Well, thank you. *(As she replaces the handset on its cradle the:)*

CURTAIN FALLS

END OF ACT ONE

A NIGHT IN OCTOBER

ACT TWO
SCENE ONE

THE SCENE *It is only a few moments after the close of the previous scene and* ANN *is still sitting at the desk wondering whether she should ring the Police or not.* RUTH *comes in from U.R. and wakens* ANN *from her worried reverie.*

RUTH: Ann, you remember you told me that there were some things of yours that you'd never be using again? In your room.
ANN: What?
RUTH: In the wardrobe in your room. A couple of summer dresses and some other things.
ANN: Oh, yes.
RUTH: Do you mind if I go in and help myself — so I can get them packed?
ANN: No. You know what they were.
RUTH: *(jocularly)* I won't take anything I'm not entitled to. I'll show you first, anyway.
ANN: No need.
RUTH: Oh, yes. Strictly above — board. Thanks a lot, Ann. *(As she moves U.R. she hears the ringing of the front door bell)* I'll see who that is. *(She goes into hall. After a moment or two she makes the announcement from the archway and then goes upstairs.)* It's Mr. Wrightson, Ann. (ANN *reacts with a start. She looks towards archway.* ROBERT *slowly enters, watching her intently, a slight smile on his face.)*
ROBERT: I've just seen Mr. Thurlow drive away.
ANN: Yes. He had to go out.

ROBERT: I upset you a bit last night. I was a bit too forthright, wasn't I?

ANN: My husband has just told me that you work for the Home Office, Mr. Wrightson.

ROBERT: Oh! Has he?

ANN: A minute ago I rang them up.

ROBERT: And they said they didn't know me.

ANN: I can't say I was surprised.

ROBERT: It takes a lot to surprise you, doesn't it?

ANN: You *did* surprise me last night. Since then I've been thinking. And I know where I was a year ago.

ROBERT: Good! I thought you'd realise you couldn't keep that up.

ANN: The night Miss Carstairs was murdered I was in London. At a hotel in Tottenham Court Road — not far from Bedford Square.

ROBERT: *(thoughtfully)* Um! *(Slight pause)* It's perfectly true that you were in London on that Friday evening, Mrs. Thurlow.

ANN: *(surprised)* You know that?

ROBERT: Of course. *(Slight pause)* But you were not at an hotel in Tottenham Court Road. From just after eight in the evening you were in the Lounge of the White Hart Hotel in Sloane Square.

ANN: Sloane Square! I don't know any hotel in Sloane Square.

ROBERT: You may not have taken any notice of the name. But you were there all right. Because it was there that you got into conversation with Derek Sheldon. You had several drinks together, didn't you?

ANN: You're making this up. Not a word of it's true.

ROBERT: Do you remember his asking if you had a car?

ANN: Certainly not. I don't remember any of it.

ROBERT: You said that you did have a car but you hadn't used it that day. You'd come up by train. You had a small blue travelling case with you. *(Slight pause)* So he brought you back here in his car.

ANN: No! This didn't happen.

ROBERT: Oh, it happened all right. Obviously you're not going to rush to admit it. But it happened. *(a little grimly)* Listen, Mrs. Thurlow, you may not be able to remember. You may not *want* to remember. But it happened and you can't go on denying it. Not for much longer, anyway.

ANN: I do deny it. And I shall go on denying it.

ROBERT: *(scornfully)* With all the proof I've got!

ANN: *(contemptuously)* Proof! What proof? You have none —
practically nothing at all. You pretend to be an official of
the Home Office. You threaten me. You put doubts in my
mind. But why, in God's name, did you pick on me?

ROBERT: I picked on you Mrs. Thurlow because it was you.

ANN: Oh, really! Is it likely I'd jeopardise everything for a
couple of hours with some man you say I picked up in a
pub?

ROBERT: I wasn't aware that adultery was the monopoly
of any one social class. (ANN *slaps his face*) I shouldn't
have said that to you. I'm sorry.

ANN: *(making a tremendous effort to be brave)* I'm not afraid
of you any more, Mr. Wrightson. *(He smiles at her.)* Nor do
I want to hear any more of your lurid fiction.

ROBERT: *(moving away D.R.)* As you please. I'll just hang
on until your husband gets back. Perhaps he'll be able to
persuade you to do the right thing. *(He sits D.R.)*

ANN: *(shaken by this threat, wonders what is the best thing
to do. Long pause. Then, finally:)* Go on.

ROBERT: You came back here and had a couple of drinks
— in this room. There was a lot of laughing and joking. You
said your name was Ann. Of course, he realised you were
married. You told him your husband was the headmaster of
Ransome's Grammar Shool. You happened to mention that
when he was appointed he was the youngest headmaster of
a Grammar School in England. (ANN *looks amazed that he
should know this*) Is that right? (ANN *doesn't answer. She
is mystified and worried.*) But you said he didn't *appreciate*
you. You loved him but his attitude to you was cold.

ANN: *(firmly)* I would never have said that. Never!

ROBERT: *(pressing on)* Derek asked where he was and you
said he'd been in Brussels since the previous Sunday and
wouldn't be back for another twenty-four hours. Didn't
you say; 'My sister's away, too. Don't worry. We're all alone?'

ANN: No, I didn't. It's a fantastic story.

ROBERT: You said you didn't care what happened because
you 'wanted to teach your husband a lesson'.

ANN: That's ridiculous. It's not like Peter and me at all.

ROBERT: Possibly not but that's what you told him. *(Pause)* When you'd finished your drinks you both went upstairs.

ANN: No. This just couldn't be true.

ROBERT: I'm getting a bit tired of you saying that, Mr. Thurlow. Good God, do you think I'm making all this up. This is what my son told me — every detail. I don't get some sort of a kick out of this. I hate it as much as you do. *(Pause)* Anyhow, when you got upstairs Derek went to the bathroom and while he was there you undressed and put on a nightdress.

ANN: Not me. No, it's all lies.

ROBERT: A flimsy little nightdress of dark blue nylon with a tiny bow of bright red ribbon at the neck. (ANN *reacts with horror. He is watching her closely.)* I daresay you know the one I'm talking about.

ANN: *(almost to herself)* I've never worn that . . . .

ROBERT: *(taking a snapshot out of his pocket and handing it to her.)* Take a look at this. (ANN *looks at the photograph, amazed and bewildered)* There was a polaroid colour camera on the table on the landing. Derek brought it into the room. There was a great deal of laughing and joking about the sort of picture he'd take.

ANN: You can't see the face.

ROBERT: No. At the last moment you got a bit panicky, didn't you? Said something about his being able to blackmail you afterwards. That's why you held that pillow up in front of your face, isn't it?

ANN: But this isn't me. It couldn't be. I've never had my photograph taken like this. I swear it.

ROBERT: Mrs. Thurlow, you were obviously upset about your husband being away, you'd had quite a lot to drink and . . . .

ANN: But I wasn't here, I tell you. I was at an hotel in London that night.

ROBERT: Which hotel, Mrs. Thurlow?

ANN: *(discomforted)* Somewhere in Tottenham Court Road — around that way.

ROBERT: Of course, you wouldn't have a billhead, receipt, card, anything?

ANN: No, I haven't. It was a year ago and . . . .

ROBERT: Of course, you haven't. Mrs. Thurlow, don't you see

what's happened? You think you did one thing whereas in
fact you did something quite different. The human mind's
a very adaptable instrument. It can prove black's white when
it wants to.

ANN: *(staring at the photo, again bewildered by it)* This couldn't
be me. I wouldn't . . . .

ROBERT: *(pointing it out to her)* Isn't that your dressing-table?
You see that large scent spray? It's still there, isn't it? Recog-
nise that silver cigarette box?
(RUTH *comes downstairs and into the room. She carries over
her arm two summer dresses and under them a dark blue
nylon nightie.)*

RUTH: *(speaking before she realises that ANN is not alone)*
These are the things you said I could have. *(She sees ROBERT)*
Oh!

ANN: Yes, yes. Take them.

RUTH: I want to make sure I've got the right ones. There's this
blue and white dress. And this brown one. And this nightie,
too. You said you didn't want it anymore.

ANN: No. No, I've never worn it. And I never shall.

RUTH: You needn't sound quite so bitter. It was a present.
What they call an unwanted gift, I suppose.

ANN: You can have it, anyway.

RUTH: Okay. Thanks. *(She goes out U.R. ROBERT smiles with
a sort of quiet triumph. ANN tries to weather the storm of
his close scrutiny.)*

ANN: *(at last)* I'd forgotten about that thing. Ruth gave it to
me as a present just after she came to live here. But I've
never worn it. It's not my style, I assure you.

ROBERT: *(taking a silver cigarette box from his pocket)* Is
this more your style?

ANN: *(staring with amazement at the box)* Where did you get
that?

ROBERT: *(reading the inscription)* For my darling husband
on our third wedding anniversary. All my love, Ann.

ANN: Where did you get it from, I asked.

ROBERT: Oh, come on now. How do you think I got it?

ANN: Somone must have stolen it and perhaps you bought it
from them and . . . .

ROBERT: I got it from Derek. And he didn't steal it. He tried to get me to buy it. But I wouldn't. We had a row and he went off in a temper and left it. The next time I saw him he was in prison.

ANN: I can't understand it. Somehow you've made up this story to fit these things. The photo and the cigarette box and . . . .

ROBERT: *(with a scornful little laugh)* I'm not as ingenious as all that. Picture me sitting there in London with a cigarette box with the name 'Ann' on it and a picture of a women in her nightie. Nothing else. And somehow I'm clairvoyant enough to know everything about you. Oh, come on!

ANN: Someone *must* have broken in here and stolen that case.

ROBERT: And got you to pose for naughty pictures while he was doing it!

ANN: But there must be an explanation.

ROBERT: Oh, there is. You gave this box to Derek that night — as a souvenir, you said.

ANN: Oh, that's a crazy idea! Do you really think I'd give away something I'd given to my husband?

ROBERT: If you wanted to score off your husband, yes. 'A woman scorned', you know.

ANN: No! No, I'd never do it.

ROBERT: Did you inform the Police that this had been stolen?

ANN: The Police? No, I . . . .

ROBERT: Why not? It's quite valuable. You treasured it.

ANN: I thought I'd mislaid it.

ROBERT: Mislaid it! Oh, that won't do. You might have told your husband that story when he noticed it was missing. *(Pause)* I daresay he'll be delighted it's turned up.

ANN: *(in horror)* What are you going to tell him?

ROBERT: I'm not looking forward to telling him anything. That's up to you. *(Pause)* In a way, I admire you. You're fighting in the only way you know to save your marriage and your husband's career. But consider the other side. Can you live with yourself when you know you could save an innocent man from spending the best years of his life in prison? Day after day you'll think about it. It will be like condemning him yourself. You won't be able to do that, will you?

ANN: *(crosses to desk and takes cheque book from drawer.)* Look! Though this story is quite untrue I shouldn't like it

to be repeated. You can't expect me to tell my husband.
And you mustn't say anything, either. *(Pause)* I have some
money — in my own account. It's not a very great deal. But
take it. I'll write you a cheque now for two thousand pounds
if you will go away and leave me alone.

ROBERT: *(sighing)* I'm no blackmailer, Mrs. Thurlow.

ANN: No, it's just that it will be better for everyone if this
story isn't repeated and . . . .

ROBERT: Mrs. Thurlow, if you offered me a million you couldn't
buy my silence. I'm fighting for a human life remember.

ANN: And what happens if you don't get your 'statement'?

ROBERT: An even messier alternative, I'm afraid. I shall give
the story to one of the Sunday newspapers. Then the Police'll
have to do something about it.

ANN: *(distraught, on point of collapse)* Can't you wait?

ROBERT: I've waited long enough.

ANN: Or have . . . . some mercy!

ROBERT: No. It's you or Derek. He's my son. You're nothing
to me. Good God, woman, what do you expect me to do?
(She collapses on desk, her head buried in her hands) I'm
going out again. *(He moves U.R.)* I'll give you an hour. Then
I'll be back. That statement had better be ready by then.
(He goes out U.R.)

CURTAIN

A NIGHT IN OCTOBER

ACT TWO
SCENE TWO

THE SCENE *is the same. It is about an hour later.* PETER *is pacing behind the settee on which a distressed* ANN *is seated.)*

PETER: *(worry making him irritable)* Well, where is he now?

ANN: He went out a little while ago. He said he'd be back in an hour . . . . for my statement.

PETER: *(comes to front of settee, sits beside* ANN *and grips her hands; grimly)* Have you told me everything, Ann? Everything?

ANN: I've told you everything he's accused me of.

PETER: Yes, but have you told me everything?

ANN: What do you mean?

PETER: The truth — the whole truth — about what really happened.

ANN: I've told you what he said happened. But that's not true. *(Desperate)* Oh, darling, surely you don't suspect . . . . for one instant . . . . that I'd do anything like that?

PETER: *(his head turned away from her; tetchily and with a slight hint of doubt)* No, no! *(Slight pause)* No, but . . . . but how could that man invent a story like that . . . . and for no reason. *(He gets up and looks at the polaroid snapshot on the desk.)* And this photograph! It does look like you. And it certainly is our bedroom.

ANN: I can't explain it. I just ask you to believe me — to believe *me*, rather than that man.

PETER: *(a flash of inspiration)* Of course. Why didn't I think of it before? Why didn't *you* think of it?

ANN: What?

PETER: Well, that week you weren't anywhere near this house, were you? *(ANN looks at him blankly)* Mabel! You spent the week with Mabel. Don't you remember that?

ANN: *(dully)* Oh, yes. Yes, I did, didn't I?

PETER: Where is she? *(ANN doesn't answer)* Come on, Ann! Where is she?

ANN: *(reluctant to give the information)* She's . . . . she's gone down to the village . . . . to the hairdressers.

PETER: Right! What we do is get her back here by the time that joker returns. I'm going to make him pay dearly, I warn you, for his slander . . . . and for upsetting you. Which hairdressers is it?

ANN: I don't know. I'm . . . . I'm not sure.

PETER: Well, there's only one, isn't there? *(He searches in the telephone directory)* That's where the yellow pages come in useful. Yes, here we are. Maison Henriques. *(He dials a number)* My God! Maison Henriques! He must have delusions of grandeur.

ANN: *(gets up and crosses to desk to prevent his completing the number)* No!

PETER: *(astonished by her action)* What do you mean, no?

ANN: I wanted her to keep quiet about it. But if it's going to come to a showdown with that man and then . . . . perhaps a court case, I can't ask her to go on . . . .

PETER: *(severely)* Ann, what are you trying to say?

ANN: *(moving away from him; with her back to him)* I didn't spend that week with Mabel.

PETER: What!

ANN: I intended to . . . . as we'd planned. I went over to Abinger. But from outside the house I could hear them having an awful row and I couldn't bring myself to go . . . . or to face a week of that sort of ting. So I came home again.

PETER: Ann! You've let me believe for a year that . . . .

ANN: It never seemed of the slightest importance until today.

PETER: And all that week I was away you spent alone in this house?

ANN: Until the Friday morning, yes.

PETER: And Ruth was away in Watford . . . . and you in your state! Whatever did you do with yourself?

ANN: I wrote.

PETER: What?

ANN: I finished my novel.

PETER: Oh, that!

ANN: I finished all the re-typing on the Thursday evening. I went up to London with it on the Friday. It was a bit late then and I didn't deliver it to the publisher's until the Saturday morning. I was a little surprised they were open, I remember.

PETER: So you spent the Friday night in London?

ANN: Yes.

PETER: All right. Where?

ANN: I don't know.

PETER: What do you mean, you don't know? You must know.

ANN: I don't. An hotel. I can't remember the name of it. And I'm not sure where it was, even. In Tottenham Court Road, I think. Somewhere around there.

PETER: *(after some thought; a bright idea)* This publisher gave you a receipt? Dated!

ANN: It was an acknowledgement printed on a small card which normally they would have posted to me.

PETER: Good! Well, where is it?

ANN: How do I know? It was a year ago. Anyway, a month or so later they returned the manuscript to me. It came by the second post when you were at school so you never knew anything about it. I daresay I destroyed the receipt at the time. There wouldn't have been any point in keeping it.

PETER: The Saturday morning you say. About what time?

ANN: When I went into Cape's? Oh, about half-past eleven, I should imagine. Perhaps a bit earlier.

PETER: *(disappointed)* Oh, well, all this doesn't help much anyway, does it?

ANN: It proves I was in London when I said and not here.

PETER: Oh, Ann, don't you see? It doesn't prove that at all.

ANN: Why not? Of course it does.

PETER: You can get from here to Bedford Square in less than an hour. You could have gone up on the Saturday morning.

ANN: But I didn't. I spent the Friday night in London, I tell you.

PETER: *(sadly)* You haven't a scrap of proof that you did.

ANN: Don't you believe me?

PETER: *(not perfectly sure whether he can believe her or not)*

Look at it from his point of view.

ANN: Whose?

PETER: That man — whoever he is. What would he say about that? That you got up on the Saturday morning feeling as guilty as hell. Your first thought was to do something which would make it look as though you hadn't been in this house on the Friday night. So you go up to London and hand in a book — which is a bit unusual, anyway — and get a dated receipt for it. This proved that you were in Bedford Square on the Saturday morning and if any questions had been asked you wanted people to draw the conclusion that you must, therefore, have been in town overnight.

ANN: But I was, I tell you.

PETER: Yet the hotel you stayed at which would have been conclusive evidence has vanished off the face of the map.

ANN: *(appalled)* Don't you believe me? Can't you bring your-self to believe me?

PETER: *(profoundly disturbed; hedging)* It isn't a question of what I believe, Ann.

ANN: *(coming to him, in desperation)* But it is. It is. Nothing else matters.

PETER: That's not true. And you know it isn't. It's what others are going to think and say.

ANN: *(despairing, hopeless)* But, Peter, if you don't believe me . . . .

PETER: Listen, Ann, when this story gets out do you think I shall be able to stay here, to carry on at the school? With people sniggering behind their palms! And you! Well, a head-master's wife has to be seen about with him. Could you put up with that, knowing that every time we appeared together in public people would be gossiping, making dirty jokes about us?

ANN: *(face hidden by her hands)* It's horrible!

PETER: You're right. It is horrible. We shall have to leave here, go to the other end of the country. Go abroad, probably. I'll be able to manage but it'll be the end of everything I've worked for all my life.

ANN: And what about us? You and me.

PETER: I can't quite see what's going to happen yet. What difference it's going to make.

ANN: *(in miserable dejection)* I can't drag you down, Peter. I love you too much. I shall go away. I shall . . . . I shall kill myself.

PETER: *(rushing to her and taking her in his arms)* No, no. You mustn't talk like that.

ANN: Oh, God, we're the victims of some hideous mistake . . . and there's nothing we can do about it.

PETER: *(gently)* Come and sit down, Ann. *(He leads her to the settee and seats her. Then moves to L. and turns.)* Ann, ask yourself, how can it be a mistake? Just imagine that condemned man sitting in his cell. It occurs to him to make up an alibi. Can you really believe that, out of the blue, he would pick on this house . . . . well, without some certainty that the story he concocted would stand up to investigation?

ANN: I told you. I've tried and tried till my head is splitting. I can't think of any explanation.

PETER: But there must be one. *(Pause)* Now listen to what I've got to say, Ann.

ANN: Yes?

PETER: Perhaps you don't realise how ill . . . . how distressed you were at that time. I know I didn't until I got back from Brussels . . . . and began to hate myself for having gone and left you alone.

ANN: I know I was on the verge of that breakdown.

PETER: Please. Afterwards when we got Sempill in you started that treatment and for a while you were very forgetful.

ANN: Yes . . . . but . . . .

PETER: Whatever you say, Ann, I don't think you can . . . . well, perhaps your memories of what happened during that week are . . . . confused.

ANN: *(thinks hard about this, obviously concluding that there might be something in what he says)* I can't bear to think that. Do you really believe that's the answer?

PETER: I wish I could think of another. But I can't. *(Slight pause)* Can you?

ANN: Have I got to believe myself capable, then – even in the wretched state I was in – of doing the things that man says I did? I can't do that. Because though I had that breakdown, through it all I know I loved you – and only you – and would never have given a thought to any other man.

PETER: Ann, you were *very* ill. You did the most incredible things at times — and then denied that you'd done them. But I am really the guilty one. I should never have forsaken you when you wanted me most. So, whatever's happened, I shall not reproach you.

ANN: *(her head held in her hands)* I must try to remember. *(slight pause)* That day I put the manuscript and my night things in the small blue case.

PETER: Did anyone see you at the station? Did you talk to anyone?

ANN: No. *(Pause)* I remember I booked in at the hotel for one night only — and I paid when I registered. *(A glimmer of hope)* I registered, darling.

PETER: Of course.

ANN: Don't you see . . . . in a hotel register . . . . *(Her hopes fade.)*

PETER: *(with a wry smile)* A pretty hopeless task if you can't even say which hotel it was.

ANN: *(crestfallen)* I didn't even use my own name.

PETER: *(perturbed by this)* What?

ANN: I felt that what I was doing was wrong. Going to London by myself when I was so ill and simply for the sake of a book I knew you wouldn't have thought very much of. I know you would have thought me a fool and . . . . this feeling of doing wrong . . . . well, I made up a name. *(Pause)* I can't remember what it was now.

PETER: *(impatiently)* You can't remember very much, can you?

ANN: I can remember having a meal in a restaurant. And I had a glass of sherry before the meal and another later on. Then I went back to the hotel and slept. I took a couple of my pills. You remember how they used to knock me out. And I can't be sure of anything else until I found myself in Bedford Square the next morning. I was carrying the case with my manuscript in it. *(A memory comes back to her vividly and she looks up at PETER almost horror-stricken.)* A man did speak to me.

PETER: What man? When?

ANN: A rather flashy young man. He followed me out of the restaurant and asked if he could give me a lift anywhere. I ignored him and walked away. *(Slight pause; almost to her-*

self) I didn't see him again.

PETER: *(shaking his head, sadly)* Darling, Ann, you're not sure of anything, are you? You told me just now that Sheldon's son reckoned that the woman he picked up had a small blue travelling case with her. Nothing else.

ANN: Yes, he did say that. *(Pause)* Is it possible then that I went to sleep in that hotel and then . . . . got up and went out . . . . and met that man? Without knowing what I was doing!

PETER: Can there be any other explanation. It's horrible, I know. For you and for me. But it's true. And we've got to face it together.

ANN: What can I do?

PETER: Ann, because you've forgotten what happened it doesn't mean that we can allow that man to languish for years in prison. Don't you see, that would be unforgiveable.

ANN: What am I going to say?

PETER: Darling, you're not in a position to deny anything he says, are you? You will have to say what his father wants you to say. Enough anyway to secure the freedom of that fellow in prison.

ANN: *(after a long pause)* I must be alone for a while. I'll go up to my room. (ANN *moves across towards doorway, and then turns.)* Is there no other way, Peter?

PETER: In your heart you know there isn't. (ANN *gives him a despairing look. He meets her gaze for a few moments, then drops his head and turns away. ANN goes. PETER sits at his desk and reads some papers. Very soon he realises that his work is no longer of importance to him and he throws the papers aside angrily. RUTH comes in. She stands looking at him for a moment or two and then crosses.)*

RUTH: I overheard what you and Ann have been saying. I was in the kitchen. I couldn't help it.

PETER: You'd know soon enough, anyway. Like everyone! The whole damned world!

RUTH: Try not to blame her too much, Peter.

PETER: It doesn't matter whether I blame her or not. The story will be out just the same.

RUTH: She couldn't have known what she was doing.

PETER: Couldn't she? I'm not so sure.

RUTH: Oh, Peter!

PETER: We had a most awful row about my going off to Brussels. She said some terrible things to me. Of course, I've forgiven her and . . . . put what she said out of my mind. I didn't realise then that she was so ill. But now I can see . . . . some of those things she said to me . . . . well, it all fits. She was going to get back at her husband . . . . that's what young Sheldon said she told him.

RUTH: She *was* very ill. Try not to think too badly of her.

PETER: My career's in ruins, I know that. I wasn't born with a silver spoon in my mouth, Ruth. Anything I've achieved has been worked for — a lifetime's hard slog. I was proud of what I'd done. I was proud of my wife. And now, in a few minutes, all destroyed. Nothing left!

RUTH: I can do something about that.

PETER: Oh, Ruth, spare me the pious condolences, please.

RUTH: Perhaps I can spare you everything.

PETER: And what does that cryptic remark mean?

RUTH: You'd be all right if Ann didn't have to make that statement.

PETER: You heard us talking. There's no choice left.

RUTH: I could say it was me.

PETER: What?

RUTH: I could say that I picked this man up in London and brought him down here because I knew the house would be empty. After all, I could have done. I've got a key.

PETER: No. It's impossible, Ruth.

RUTH: I could say that I left Watford early — say on the Friday afternoon — absolutely fed up with myself because of the way things had turned out. And I went into this pub — it doesn't matter that I can't remember the name — to drown my sorrows. And I got into conversation with this chap . . . .

PETER: *(not impressed with the idea)* And you told him your name was Ann and that your husband was a headmaster attending a conference in Brussels. And you put on Ann's nightdress and used our bed and gave away my silver cigarette box as a keepsake! That's a bit too far-fetched for anyone to believe, isn't it?

RUTH: Perhaps, normally. But think! I'm engaged to be married — in a few days' time to a very respectable man. Doesn't that put me in the same position as Ann? Would any woman make such a sacrifice — except for the truth?

PETER: You're excited, Ruth. Please, think about what you're saying.

RUTH: And you think about it, too, Peter. Very carefully.

PETER: But . . . . you were in Watford. I mean, the Macaulays know that.

RUTH: You don't think that man will check that part of the story, do you? All he's interested in is getting a statement that his son was *otherwise engaged* on the night of the murder.

PETER: *(after thinking about the plan for a moment or two)* No, Ruth, no. I can't let you do it.

RUTH: Why not? I listened to every word that passed between you and Ann just now. The story could easily apply to me. I even borrowed the case — the next biggest one — from that new set you bought. Similar to the one Ann took to London. I wouldn't have to lie much. It would be easy for me.

PETER: But you wouldn't have used Ann's name or our bed.

RUTH: Oh, I don't know. What more natural than the poor sister pretending to be the mistress of the house, laying claim to her famous husband, using her clothes and her bed when she had the chance?

PETER: But it's such a sordid story. The scandal will be awful. Think of your marriage, Ruth.

RUTH: The scandal for me won't be pleasant. But it would *ruin* you, Peter. And you've so much more to lose than I have. I've been in scrapes before, goodness •only knows. I expect I shall weather the storm. *(Slight pause)* And I have thought about my marriage.

PETER: Well?

RUTH: I'd like you to do something about that for me.

PETER: What can I possibly do?

RUTH: Go and see Jonathan and tell him what I'm doing and why. Tell him the whole truth. That won't be easy for you. But tell him. I don't think he'd disapprove. In any case, the scandal won't touch us much. After the wedding we're going to Spain to live.

PETER: *(wavering)* You'll have to give me a little time to think about it.

RUTH: There is no time. That man will be back any minute now to collect his statement. And from what I heard he's not likely to be put off for much longer. Oh, for God's sake, Peter, save yourself.

PETER: *(thinks about it, then turns away)* No, no. It's too much for anyone to do.

RUTH: But I *want* to do it.

PETER: Want to?

RUTH: *(going close to him)* I can't stand by and see everything you've worked for in ruins. If this story is made public it will be like dying for you. Either the end of everything or you'll have to go right away and start from scratch again. Honestly, it doesn't mean so much to me *(she lifts her hand to his face and touches it gently)* In any case, Peter, you can't stop me.

PETER: What do you mean? *(He is affected by her tenderness and holds her hand against his cheek with affection.)*

RUTH: When this Mr. Sheldon — or Mr. Wrightson — comes back I shall openly tell him what he want to hear and you'll be standing there and you won't dare stop me.

PETER: *(after a little while)* Why should you sacrifice yourself, Ruth. We've treated you like a servant and yet . . . .

RUTH: There's a simple answer to that, Peter. Simple but the best in the world. *(Pause)* I love you.

PETER: *(he holds her. a long pause. He looks into her eyes)* I know, Ruth. I suppose I've known all along.

RUTH: Kiss me. Just once.
(They kiss. After a little while he tries to break away but she holds him to the kiss for a long time. Finally, they draw apart.)
You can't know what happiness there is for me in doing this. If you're all right, Peter, then so am I. So, no more arguments. Get Ann down and . . . . break the good news to her.

PETER: *(a final moment of indecision. Then, turning to the doorway)* Yes. *(He turns back at doorway to her)* I shall never forget you . . . . for this, Ruth.

RUTH: *(with a slight smile)* I hope not.
(PETER goes out and upstairs. RUTH smiles with self-satisfaction. She goes to the desk and begins to write out her 'confession'. The front door is heard to close. MABEL comes into the room.)

MABEL: Well, how do I look? Glamorous?

RUTH: *(quickly glancing up and then returning to her writing)*
Spectacular!

MABEL: This is really the final exercise in seduction. It it doesn't
work . . . . Oh, but it's got to. I can't afford to fail this time.

RUTH: *(disinterested)* I know exactly how you feel.

MABEL: *(standing in front of mirror, admiring herself)* There was
a bit of excitement when I was in the hairdressers. Monsieur
Henriques — by the way, I learnt his real name in Henry
Stubbs — got himself in quite a tizzy.

RUTH: Oh?

MABEL: The Police were digging up the garden of one of the
cottages on the other side of the road.

RUTH: Does Monsieur Henriques bury his dissatisfied clients
there?

MABEL: No. They were after stolen goods.

RUTH: I know they found Peter's microscopes and medals.
That's old news.

MABEL: They found a lot of other things as well. Apparently
the man who lives there — his name's Swann and he's a motor
mechanic — has done quite a few jobs in the neighbourhood.

RUTH: 'Done quite a few jobs!' Oh, the jargon!

MABEL: I pick it up from Z-cars. Anyway, he buries his loot
in his garden — by dead of night, I imagine — until he can
sell it off.

RUTH: That's very intriguing, Mabel. But I'm trying to write.

MABEL: *(huffily)* Sorry! *(She turns to go.)*

RUTH: *(stopping her with her voice)* Wait! I think you ought
to know about this.

MABEL: What?

RUTH: I'm not going into details but . . . . well, it's necessary
for me to say that I was in this house on the night of October
the third last year. That's the night that Miss Carstairs was
murdered, and it's got something to do with that.

MABEL: What are you up to, Ruth? It sounds a bit scarey to me.

RUTH: You know I wasn't here. But I'm going to say I was to
save Peter. So don't open this. *(She indicates her mouth.)*

MABEL: *(put out a bit)* I suppose you're entitled to your secrets
. . . . but I *am* your sister.

RUTH: Just don't say anything when that man comes back.
Got me? Not a word!

MABEL: Oh, all right! I wouldn't say anything to that man, anyway. He gives me the shivers.

(ANN *and* PETER *are heard coming down stairs.* MABEL *goes out. In the hallway* PETER *says: 'Oh, you're back, Mabel'.* MABEL *is heard hurrying upstairs. The front door bell rings.)*

PETER: *(off)* That'll be our friend. (ANN *comes into the room.* PETER *has gone to open front door.)*

ANN: *(crossing to desk)* Peter's told me. Why should you?

PETER: *(off)* Come on in.

RUTH: Don't say anything about it. Not a word. My mind's made up. *(She continues writing.* ANN *draws away to french windows, watching* RUTH *intently.* PETER *and* ROBERT *enter from hall.)*

ROBERT: *(to* PETER) You were out when I spoke to Mrs. Thurlow just now.

PETER: She told me. As soon as I got back. Everything.

ROBERT: Did she? Well, I'm sorry. It's a miserable business. But if you had a son you'd fight for him, wouldn't you?

PETER: *(shortly)* I suppose so.

ROBERT: Now it's out in the open . . . . *(Turns to* ANN) Mrs. Thurlow, have you done what I asked?

RUTH: *(looking up from her writing)* I've nearly finished, Mr. Sheldon.

ROBERT: You? *(Pause. He is baffled)* But . . . . wait a minute. I don't understand.

RUTH: This should be enough to get your son out of prison. That's what you want, isn't it?

ROBERT: *(looking from* ANN *to* RUTH *and back; suspicious; not quite certain what has happened)* My God, so you've worked it between you!

RUTH: No, there's no mystery. You just weren't very careful with your investigations, that's all. Perhaps you weren't so wise to take the law into your own hands. The innocent are likely to get hurt that way.

ROBERT: Let's see what you've written. *(He crosses to desk and reads over her shoulder.)* Yes. Yes, that's everything. *(Looking intently at* RUTH) But Derek was so sure it was Mrs. ANN Thurlow. You must have told him that was your name.

RUTH: *(perkily)* Yes, I did.

ROBERT: *(chastened; thoughtfully)* It just shows you how easy it is to be deceived. Like last night. When I got knocked over by that car I assumed it would be driven by Mrs. Thurlow. If I'd left this house before I'd found out my mistake I'd have gone into a court of law swearing it. *(Turns to* ANN) I can only say that . . . . Well, I got the story from Derek. How was he to know that someone had lied to him about her name?

PETER: Let's hear no more about it, Mr. Sheldon. Take your statement and go.

ROBERT: Yes. *(He looks again over* RUTH'S *shoulder)* Sign it.

RUTH: *(signs the paper)* There! Now my conscience is clear.

ROBERT: *(takes statement and reads it through)* Thank you. *(As he turns away indecisively, as though he ought to say something in extenuation,* ANN *catches the look exchanged between* RUTH *and* PETER. *She looks thoughtful for a moment and then speaks just in time to stop* ROBERT *leaving the room.)*

ANN: *(sharply)* Mr. Sheldon! Wait a minute, please.

PETER: What is it, Ann. Haven't we finished with this wretched business?

ANN: It looks as if your son will be pardoned now . . . . and released.

ROBERT: I don't know how long these things take. I shall do everything I can to hurry it through now. Perhaps a week or two . . . . I don't know.

ANN: Would you do me a favour?

ROBERT: *(surprised and embarrassed)* Well, yes. If I can.

ANN: I think you owe it to me.

ROBERT: Yes. What is it?

ANN: As soon as your son is released would you ask him to come down here and see me.

PETER: *(annoyed)* Ann, what are you up to?

ROBERT: You really want that?

ANN: Yes, Mr. Sheldon. Very much.

PETER: What good is it going to do, Ann? If he agrees to come — which I very much doubt — it will be horrible for him and for you.

ANN: I'd like him to come and see me all the same. And I'd like you and Ruth to be here.

RUTH: I don't want to meet him.

ANN: Naturally.

PETER: Ann, will you drop this nonsense at once, please?

ANN: No, I won't. Because you, Peter, believe what Mr. Sheldon has told you about me.

PETER: Please stop. It'll do no good raking it all over again.

ANN: And you believe Ruth is making the great sacrifice of her reputation and her honour to save us the scandal!

PETER: Yes, I do. And it would be more becoming, Ann, if you showed her a little gratitude.

RUTH: *(with bitterness)* I'm not doing it for you, Ann. Only for Peter.

PETER: Now, Ann, please. Don't work yourself up again.

ANN: *(to* ROBERT*)* If you walk out of here now with that paper, Mr. Sheldon, my husband will go on believing what he's been told. And I shan't have any way of showing him where the truth is. *(Slight pause)* Every word Ruth has written in that statement is true. I've no doubt about that. In the end she probably had to salve her conscience.

RUTH: *(bitterly)* I knew I might get this from you.

ANN: Most of what happened to me a year ago I can't be sure of. But here and there — some things; quite trivial things, sometimes — are crystal clear.

PETER: Well?

ANN: Ever since Mr. Sheldon spoke to me last night I've been trying to . . . . to penetrate my memory of . . . . of that Friday evening. But I can't. Nothing more than what I've already told you. I don't suppose I shall ever know now what really happened after I booked in at that hotel.

PETER: *(kindly)* We understand, Ann.

ANN: But a few minutes ago it occurred to me that I was making a big mistake.

PETER: What do you mean? Mistake!

ANN: I ought not to be concentrating on the things I knew I could never remember but giving all my attention to those things I could remember quite clearly. And that's what I was doing up in my bedroom just now.

PETER: Look, Ann, I can't see what you're getting at. If something's come back to you about that Friday night . . . .

ANN: Not the Friday night, no. But the afternoon.

PETER: Eh?

ANN: Just before I took my book up to London. I remember it absolutely clearly.

PETER: What?

ANN: I went up to the bedroom to get the small case to put my book in and, as I was about to leave I looked down at my unmade bed. I was about to make it when I . . . . and I remember this quite clearly . . . . I told myself, jokingly, that a great novelist wouldn't bother about such details. And I walked away.

PETER: Oh, come on, Ann. What's all this leading to?

ANN: Simply this. When I got back here on the Saturday afternoon, the bed had been made.

RUTH: What do you want me to say? That I made it? I'm doing enough already to save your marriage.

ANN: If I didn't make it there is only one other person, Ruth, who would have done. The person who usually made it.

RUTH: You're forgetting one thing, Ann. I came in after you.

ANN: I've been thinking about that. Couldn't you have gone out and waited until you were sure I was home?

RUTH: Peter, you know the truth. Tell her.

ANN: He doesn't know the truth. Only the stories he's been told. *(Slight pause)* There's another thing. When did you leave Watford, Ruth?

RUTH: I've told you. On the Saturday morning. Late on the Saturday morning.

ANN: You told me once that after that debacle with Tom Macaulay you got — what you called 'sloshed'. You rather boasted that you'd drunk half a bottle of whisky to drown your sorrows. Well, you weren't 'sloshed' when you walked in here on the Saturday afternoon, were you? Shall I tell you when you drowned your sorrows, Ruth? In a pub in Sloane Square on the Friday night. And that's where Mr. Sheldon's son picked you up.

RUTH: Peter, it's wrong that she should turn on me when I made that statement for one reason only — to save you trouble.

ANN: That can all be settled when young Mr. Sheldon comes down here. I'm sure he'll be able to say which one of us he spent the night with.

RUTH: *(defiant)* I shouldn't think you'd be able to look him in the face. And I certainly don't want to see him.

ANN: In that case I shall go up to London to see him. Perhaps you'd like to come to London with me, Ruth?

RUTH: *(rising angrily)* I've had enough of this. I'm going up to my room. I did what I said I'd do, Peter. Now, as far as I'm concerned, the whole thing is over. *(She crosses towards doorway and as she passes* ROBERT *who has been standing on the threshold of the room fascinated but baffled by the confrontation of the sisters, she unexpectedly snatches the 'confession' from his hand and begins to tear it up.* ROBERT *struggles with her and finally retrieves the torn paper.)*

PETER: Ruth, what are you . . . . ?

RUTH: *(turning, snarling)* Oh, leave me alone. *(Turning on* ANN*)* You look so smug. Because you've always got what you wanted out of life without making the slightest effort. All my life I've had to fight for what *I* wanted. And still I never got it. *(She looks at* PETER*)* But for one night I did. Or near it. For one night, Ann, I was you, in your house, in your bed. I even pretended that man was Peter. What do you think of that? *(She rushes out of the room and upstairs.)*

ROBERT: *(after some time, looking at the torn paper in his hands)* I daresay this will do. In any case, we all heard what she said.

MABEL: *(entering)* Whatever's the matter with Ruth?

PETER: *(hesitantly)* We had a bit of a row.

MABEL: Oh, Peter, you shouldn't. She's taken it very badly. Just rushed by me on the stairs crying her eyes out.

PETER: She'll get over it.

MABEL: *(after a slight pause)* What I came down to tell you . . . I've just heard it on the local radio. That young man who stole the stuff from your school . . . . well the Police have found some of the stuff stolen from Miss Carstairs' house and . . . . He's helping police with enquiries into the murder, as they say.

ROBERT: *(with sudden, excited resolution crosses to phone without asking anyone's permission)* Police! *(Spoken in phone after dialling 999. Pause.)* I want to speak to the officer in charge of the Carstairs' murder enquiry. I expect it'll be Chief Inspector Mansell. Yes, it's very important. *(Waits)*

Oh, hello, Chief Inspector. Robert Sheldon here. You remember me? *(He listens.)* Thank God for that! A wonderful relief! Yes, I understand you can't say any more. But that's enough. Thank you very much. Goodbye. *(He hangs up and turns to the others.)* The Police have found the man who killed Miss Carstairs. It seems he's admitted it. *(He tears up what remains of the 'confession' and crosses to doorway. He turns.)* It's a cruel irony, isn't it? I purposely came down here on the anniversary of the murder. I don't know, it was just a super-stition. If I'd waited one more day I could have . . . . saved you all this . . . . this worry. *(A wry smile)* I'm truly sorry. But I wasn't to know, was I?

(ROBERT *goes out.* MABEL *stands indecisively for a moment or two, looking from* PETER *to* ANN, *and then realises she is superfluous. She goes out and we hear her going upstairs. There is an awkward, tense pause.* ANN *is not facing* PETER.)

PETER: *(at last; brokenly, uncertain)* I doubted you. *(Pause)* I was swept along, Ann, I . . . . *(pause)* I'll have to start all over again to show that I really love you. *(Pause)* Can you . . . . can you forgive me? (ANN *turns slowly, a slight enigmatic smile on her face)* Can you? .

ANN: I don't know. *(Pause)* I don't know. But . . . . I'll try. Of course, I'll try.

CURTAIN

A NIGHT IN OCTOBER

LIGHTING PLOT

Apparent sources of light: By day: daylight through french
windows L.

By night: Pendant in living-room.
Brackets in living-room (if
available)
Pendant in Hall.
Reading-lamp on desk.

ACT ONE. Scene 1. Late evening.

To open: Room in semi-darkness, lit only by gloom from Garden L.

Cue 1.   Key heard in front door. Slight pause. Hall light ON.
(Page 5.)

Cue 2.   ROBERT (off): No, no. It's not that bad.
As Mabel enters. All lights except desk-lamp ON.
(Page 5.)

ACT ONE. Scene 2. About 8.30 am. Bright, sunny day.

Room is lit by bright sunshine from windows L.

ACT TWO. Scene 1. The same.

ACT TWO. Scene 2. The same.

A NIGHT IN OCTOBER

EFFECTS PLOT

ACT ONE. Scene 1.

As curtain rises: distant rumble of thumder.	(Page 5)
Key heard in lock. Front door opens and is closed.	(Page 5)
MABEL hurries out U.R. Clap of thunder, nearer than before.	(Page 9)
MABEL goes into hall, followed by ROBERT. Low rumble of thunder. Front door opens and closes.	(Page 11)
ROBERT: Look, would you be good enough to tie this handkerchief around my elbow. A vivid flash of lightning and rumble of thunder.	(Page 13)
ROBERT: . . . but at first mistook her for you. Flash of lightning and thunder.	(Page 14)
Front door is heard to close, before PETER enters.	(Page 14)
PETER: You did what? I see. Rumble of thunder and torrential rain.	(Page 15)
ANN: *(laughing)* Granted! The telephone rings.	(Page 19)
ANN crosses to french windows. Torrential rain against glass. Vivid lightning.	(Page 19)
ANN: . . . to convince yourself it wasn't your fault. Lightning and thunder, almost simultaneously.	(Page 21)
ANN, alone, after MABEL'S exit. Telephone rings.	(Page 21)

ROBERT looks upstairs.
A loud rumble of thunder. (Page 29)

ACT ONE. Scene 2.

ROBERT exits. Telephone rings. (Page 39)

MABEL exits. Telephone rings. (Page 40)

ACT TWO. Scene 1.

No effects.

ACT TWO. Scene 2.

PETER exits. Front door is heard to close. (Page 63)

PETER: *(off)* Oh, you're back, Mabel.
Front door bell rings. (Page 65)

A NIGHT IN OCTOBER

PROPERTY PLOT

On Stage: Two or three books on small table D.R.
Cushions in armchairs and on settee.
Magazine on settee.
Drinks Table: Brandy, whisky, sherry, grape-fruit juice (small bottles). Glasses, Syphon. Small vase of flowers.
Small book case U.L. Books and telephone directories.
Desk: on it, lamp, telephone, inkstand, pen, pencils, paper, envelopes, books, photo of PETER in leather frame.
in it: in drawer, cheque book (ANN'S)
Small table D.L. On it: Vase of flowers.
On walls: Good quality reproductions of modern paintings, possibly, Mondrian, Magritte, Modigliani portraits (not nudes); prints. Various ornaments.

ACT ONE.
Scene 1.   Cape, handbag with lipstick and small mirror. (ANN)
Handkerchief, photograph from newspaper. (ROBERT)
Brief case containing papers and books. (PETER)

ACT ONE
Scene 2.

Off: Two cups of coffee on small tray (for RUTH)
Jacket in hall (for PETER)

Dressing-gown, letters (PETER)
Apron, duster (RUTH)

On Stage: Newspapers on coffee table behind settee.

ACT TWO.
Scene 1.

Polaroid snapshot, small silver cigarette case.
(ROBERT)
Two summer dressers and short blue nylon night-dress with red ribbon (off) for RUTH.

ACT TWO.
Scene 2.

Polaroid snapshot on desk.

NOTES

NOTES

NOTES

NOTES

NOTES